The Vietnam War

by Roger Barr

America's WARS

Lucent Books, P.O. Box 289011, San Diego, CA 92198-0011

Books in the America's Wars Series:

The Revolutionary War

The Indian Wars

The War of 1812

The Mexican-American War

The Civil War

The Spanish-American War

World War I

World War II: The War in the Pacific

World War II: The War in Europe

The Korean War

The Vietnam War

The Persian Gulf War

Library of Congress Cataloging-in-Publication Data

Barr, Roger, 1951–

The Vietnam War / by Roger Barr.

p.   cm. — (America's wars)

Includes bibliographical references and index.

Summary: Discusses the course of the Vietnam War from its early stages before American involvement to the 1974 ceasefire and its aftermath.

ISBN 1-56006-410-2

1. Vietnamese Conflict, 1961–1975—Juvenile literature.
[1. Vietnamese Conflict. 1961–1975.]   I. Title.   II. Series.

DS557.7.B36 1991

959.704'3—dc20   91-23067

Contents

Foreword

War, justifiable or not, is a descent into madness. George Washington, America's first president and commander-in-chief of its armed forces, wrote that his most fervent wish was "to see this plague of mankind, war, banished from the earth." Most, if not all of the forty presidents who succeeded Washington have echoed similar sentiments. Despite this, not one generation of Americans since the founding of the republic has been spared the maelstrom of war. In its brief history of just over two hundred years, the United States has been a combatant in eleven major wars. And four of those conflicts have occurred in the last fifty years.

America's reasons for going to war have differed little from those of most nations. Political, social, and economic forces were at work which either singly or in combination ushered America into each of its wars. A desire for independence motivated the Revolutionary War. The fear of annihilation led to the War of 1812. A related fear, that of having the nation divided, precipitated the Civil War. The need to contain an aggressor nation brought the United States into the Korean War. And territorial ambition lay behind the Mexican-American and the Indian Wars. Like all countries, America, at different times in its history, has been victimized by these forces and its citizens have been called to arms.

Whatever reasons may have been given to justify the use of military force, not all of America's wars have been popular. From the Revolutionary War to the Vietnam War, support of the people has alternately waxed and waned. For example, less than half of the colonists backed America's war of independence. In fact, most historians agree that at least one-third were committed to maintaining America's colonial status. During the Spanish-American War, a strong antiwar movement also developed. Resistance to the war was so high that the Democratic party made condemning the war a significant part of its platform in an attempt to lure voters into voting Democratic. The platform stated that "the burning issue of imperialism growing out of the Spanish war involves the very existence of the Republic and the destruction of our free institutions." More recently, the Vietnam War divided the nation like no other conflict had since the Civil War. The mushrooming antiwar movements in most major cities and colleges throughout the United States did more to bring that war to a conclusion than did actions on the battlefield.

Yet, there have been wars which have enjoyed overwhelming public support. World Wars I and II were popular because people believed that the survival of America's democratic institutions was at stake. In both wars, the American people rallied with an enthusiasm and spirit of self-sacrifice that was remarkable for a country with such a diverse population. Support for food and fuel rationing, the purchase of war bonds, a high rate of voluntary enlistments, and countless other forms of voluntarism, were characteristic of the people's response to those wars. Most recently, the Persian Gulf War prompted an unprecedented show of support even though the United States was not directly threatened by the conflict. Rallies in support of U.S. troops were widespread. Tens of thousands of individuals, including families, friends, and well-wishers of the troops sent packages of food, cosmetics, clothes, cassettes, and suntan oil. And even more supporters wrote letters to unknown soldiers that were forwarded to the military front. In fact, most public opinion polls revealed that up to 90 percent of all Americans approved of their nation's involvement.

The complex interplay of events and purposes that leads to military conflict should be included in a history of any war. A simple chronicling of battles and casualty lists at best offers only a partial history of war. Wars do not spontaneously erupt; nor does their memory perish. They are driven by underlying causes, fueled by policymakers, fought and supported by citizens, and remembered by those plotting a nation's future. For these reasons wars, or the fear of wars, will always leave an indelible stamp on any nation's history and influence its future.

The purpose of this series is to provide a full understanding of America's Wars by presenting each war in a historical context. Each of the twelve volumes focuses on the events that led up to the war, the war itself, its impact on the home front, and its aftermath and influence upon future conflicts. The unique personalities, the dramatic acts of courage and compassion, as well as the despair and horror of war are all presented in this series. Together, they show why America's wars have dominated American consciousness in the past as well as how they guide many political decisions of today. In these vivid and objective accounts, students will gain an understanding of why America became involved in these conflicts, and how historians, military and government officials, and others have come to understand and interpret that involvement.

Chronology of Events

1883
France establishes total control over Vietnam, ending its independence.

1930
Ho Chi Minh organizes Indochinese Communist party.

September 2, 1945
Ho Chi Minh declares Vietnam independent.

March 6, 1946
Vietnam and France agree Vietnam is a free state within French Union, but agreement soon falls apart.

December 19, 1946
Ho Chi Minh calls for war against France.

May 7, 1954
French surrender to the Communists at Dien Bien Phu.

May-July 1954
Geneva Conference held; Vietnam formally separated into North and South Vietnam.

January 1, 1955
United States starts to aid Ngo Dinh Diem's South Vietnam government.

November 22, 1961
United States decides to expand military aid and advisers to South Vietnam. U.S. personnel raised to 3,200 by end of year.

August 2-4, 1964
North Vietnamese attack U.S. warships *Maddox* and *Turner Joy* in Gulf of Tonkin. Johnson orders first U.S. air strikes against North Vietnam on August 4.

August 7, 1964
Congress passes Gulf of Tonkin Resolution.

March 1965
First U.S. combat troops sent to Vietnam.

October 1967
Forty thousand protest the war at the Pentagon.

January 30, 1968
Tet Offensive begins.

March 10, 1968
U.S. poll shows 49 percent of Americans think U.S. involvement in the war is a mistake.

March 31, 1968
Johnson offers to negotiate with the North Vietnamese for peace; announces he will not run for reelection.

June 8, 1969
President Nixon announces first U.S. troop withdrawal of 25,000. Withdrawals continue for next four years.

April 30, 1970
U.S. and South Vietnam invade Cambodia.

May 4, 1970
During nationwide protests, four students killed at Kent State University in Ohio. Ten days later two students killed at Jackson State University in Mississippi.

February 8, 1971
South Vietnamese troops backed by U.S. Air Force invades Laos.

Spring 1972
North Vietnam launches Spring Offensive against South Vietnam.

Summer 1972
Serious negotiations begin between North Vietnam and the United States.

January 27, 1973
Paris Peace Accords signed, ending U.S. military involvement in Vietnam. Fighting between North and South Vietnam soon resumes.

November 7, 1973
Congress passes War Powers Act over Nixon's veto, preventing future presidents from sending U.S. troops overseas for more than sixty days without congressional approval.

August 9, 1974
Nixon resigns as president of the United States over Watergate scandal.

April 30, 1975
Saigon falls to the Communists. Last Americans leave U.S. embassy.

INTRODUCTION

A Painful Lesson that Should Be Remembered

Throughout history, war has followed a similar pattern. Peoples or countries disagree, they fight with the weapons of the times, and people die. One side wins, the other loses. Yet the circumstances surrounding each war are unique—and each is somehow different from the rest.

Except for the Civil War, the Vietnam War divided the United States like no other war. While Vietnam did not divide the country into North and South, as the Civil War had done, both wars divided America psychologically. The Civil War pitted brother against brother, and national loyalty was split between loyalty to country and one's way of life. The Vietnam War split Americans into war supporters and war protesters and also set them against each other.

The legacy of Vietnam and what it means to America still divides American opinion to this day, which makes generalizations about the war difficult. In 1991, when America participated in the Persian Gulf War, every decision was debated against the backdrop of the Vietnam War. From whether the United States should become involved to how returning soldiers should be treated, Vietnam provided the example for how the United States was not going to act. In many ways the Persian Gulf War showed just how deeply Vietnam had permanently scarred the American conscience.

The Vietnam War radically changed America. The America that withdrew from Vietnam in 1973 was a much different country from the one that, in 1964, committed troops to Vietnam to stop the spread of communism. Because of Vietnam, Americans reevaluated themselves and their country's morality and motives. Americans also came to the painful realization that they could not automatically trust elected officials. These changes still influence America today and probably will for many years to come.

There are usually more lessons to be found in failure than in success. America committed many political and military mistakes in the Vietnam War, and each mistake can be viewed as a lesson. Critics remain divided about what the true lessons of Vietnam are, but nearly everyone agrees that another Vietnam is an experience that America must avoid. Indeed, the desire to avoid another Vietnam may be the most important part of a complicated and contradictory legacy that Vietnam has left America.

CHAPTER ONE

How the United States Became Entangled in Vietnam

The seeds that grew into the United States' tangled political and military involvement in Vietnam in the 1960s were sown at the end of World War II. The war had destroyed the old world order. The colonial system, where nations maintained control over other countries or territories, was almost completely destroyed by the war.

The United States had emerged from the chaos of World War II as one of the most powerful nations in the world. As the process of rebuilding the world began, America's leaders looked back on their country's successful role in defeating the Germans and the Japanese and concluded that the United States was powerful enough to hold its own against any nation in the world. America's leaders believed the United States should influence and guide the governments of other countries. For the future safety of the United States and the world, every country should develop economic and strategic policies sympathetic to the interests of the United States, these leaders concluded.

This ambitious goal became one of the cornerstones of America's foreign policy in the decade after World War II. The spread of communism around the world, however, almost immediately challenged that goal.

Communism is a system where all property and businesses are owned by the government. In theory, workers work for the government and in return receive everything they need to live, including a home, food, health care, and guaranteed employment. Communism is the opposite of capitalism, in which most of the property is owned privately by people or corporations.

One of the principles, or doctrines, of communism is that as the world evolves, more and more nations will become Communist. Through revolutions, communism is supposed to eventually take over the world.

The spread of communism was perceived by America's leaders as a threat to U.S. national security. Since it was the opposite of the American system, Communist countries were not likely to have economic and strategic policies that favored the United States. In addition, U.S. leaders believed in a phenomenon called the domino theory. This theory stated that if one nation became Communist, the surrounding nations might also fall, just like dominoes, to communism.

If America allowed this to happen, Communist countries might take over the world. America's postwar leaders wanted to create a democratic world, and communism prevented that possibility.

The Soviet Union had become the world's first Communist nation in 1918. The Soviet Union, like the United States, was trying to spread its ideology, communism. Its goal directly conflicted with the world the United States sought to build. Although the United States and the Soviet Union had been forced to become allies to defeat Germany in World War II, after the war ended, the two nations became bitter enemies. The Soviet Union set up Communist-led puppet governments in the Eastern European countries it had occupied at the end of the war. This move angered U.S. officials, who wanted the nations to detemine their own destiny through national elections that would favor the United States.

These two great world powers struggled to get more nations to adopt their ideologies. This conflict became known as the cold war. Since other nations either aligned with the United States or the Soviet Union, the cold war dominated world politics.

The purpose of American foreign policy was dominated by winning the cold war through containing the spread of communism. In 1947, President Harry S Truman announced a new American policy intended to contain communism in Southeastern Europe. Truman promised that America would support, through military and economic aid, all free peoples resisting communism.

The United States successfully used this policy, known as the Truman Doctrine, to help the Greek people oppose communism in a civil war. The United States also aided Turkey at the end of World War II. These successes helped increase America's confidence that it could reconstruct the world to its own advantage.

The Spread of Communism

The United States also saw communism as a growing threat in Asia, halfway around the world. Korea had already been divided

President Harry S Truman promised military and economic aid to countries that opposed the spread of communism.

In 1931, members of the French Foreign Legion smashed a rebellion led by the Indochinese Communist party.

into a Communist North and a pro-American South. In China, Communists had been struggling to gain control of their country for more than twenty years. In Southeast Asia, Communists were working against the established governments in several countries. A similar struggle was occurring between Vietnamese Communists and French colonialists in Vietnam. In order to contain the threat of communism, the United States chose to support France in the bitter struggle.

Vietnam's Struggle for Independence

The struggle between the Vietnamese and the French for control of Vietnam had begun long before a Communist party even existed in Vietnam. Vietnam had been an important French colony for nearly a century. The French had first established missions in Vietnam during the eighteenth century. The French ruled Vietnam harshly. In their own country, Vietnamese people were prohibited from traveling outside their districts without identification papers. They were not allowed to attend public meetings, nor could they organize or publish newspapers. They were subject to forced labor and could be imprisoned by the order of any French magistrate.

Ho Chi Minh: Most Enlightened One

Ho Chi Minh (1890-1969) is the most important figure in Vietnam's long struggle for independence. From the most humble of beginnings, Ho rose to become the leader of his country. He was the architect for the Communists' fifty-year struggle to free Vietnam from foreign control. Many facts about his life have been clouded by his secret activities and by his use of aliases, or made-up names, to protect his identity. His original name was Nguyen That Thanh or Nguyen Van Thanh. He adopted the name Ho Chi Minh, meaning "most enlightened one," in the 1940s.

Ho traveled widely in his early years, settling in Paris in 1918, the same year the Communists overthrew the Russian government. Ho became a Communist, and for the next fifty years, worked to free his country from control by the French, the Japanese, and the United States.

His life as a revolutionary and liberator was not an easy one. He was sentenced to death by the French in 1929 because of his anti-French activities. In 1930, he was imprisoned briefly by the British and in 1941 he was arrested by the Chinese on charges of being a French spy.

Despite these setbacks, Ho was successful where Vietnamese leaders before him had failed. He understood that the success of any revolution in Vietnam depended upon the support of the Vietnamese peasants. Upon his return to Vietnam during World War II, Ho and his forces set about organizing the peasants.

Ho's practicality was another reason for his success. Unlike his predecessors, he was willing to compromise and even make temporary allies of his foes in his quest to free Vietnam. This strategy allowed him to fight on his own terms and on his own schedule rather than on that of his enemies.

Ho died in 1969, six years before the reunification of North and South Vietnam. For his role in Vietnam's struggle for freedom, Ho is a hero to the Vietnamese people, who affectionately still refer to him as "Uncle Ho."

Ho Chi Minh led the Vietnamese struggle for independence from foreign control. Many Vietnamese people today remember him as a hero.

Japanese cycling troops pass through Saigon in this photograph taken after the Japanese invaded Vietnam.

Although the Vietnamese bristled under French rule, no leader was able to rally the support necessary to mount a successful revolution against the French. In 1930, however, a Vietnamese leader appeared who would become a key figure in Vietnam's quest for independence. His name was Ho Chi Minh. Not only was Ho a nationalist who favored Vietnamese independence, he was also a Communist. He had studied communism in France and the Soviet Union during the 1920s before returning to Southeast Asia.

In 1930, Ho helped to unify three small Communist parties under the name of the Indochinese Communist Party (ICP). The new party's objectives, which Ho drafted, included the overthrow of the French and the establishment of Vietnamese independence.

The ICP's first attempt to establish Vietnamese independence met with failure. In 1930, the new party helped organize workers and peasants to protest worsening economic conditions in two of Vietnam's provinces. When their demands were not met, the peaceful demonstrations turned into riots. The French Foreign Legion squelched the rebellion in early 1931.

Through most of the 1930s, the ICP worked at rebuilding itself. Ho spent much of the decade in Moscow studying and teaching.

The Struggle Against French Rule

While the United States was fighting Germany and Japan during World War II, the Vietnamese Communists continued their struggle to free Vietnam from French rule. World War II complicated their struggle. In 1940, Japan took advantage of the fact that France was fighting in Europe and invaded portions of Vietnam. Instead of having one foreign country to fight against for independence, Ho suddenly had two.

The Japanese urged the Vietnamese to support them against the French. Although the Vietnamese Communists did not trust the Japanese, they used Japan's invasion as an opportunity to seize French-held lands. But France and Japan soon arranged a cease-fire, and the French returned and regained the territories the Communists had seized.

Ho returned to Vietnam in early 1941, after being absent from his homeland for thirty years. For three decades, he had directed Vietnamese revolutionary activities from other countries to avoid being arrested by the French. He set up new headquarters in a cave in the northern part of Vietnam, near the Chinese border. From his new headquarters, Ho met with Vietnamese Communists to establish the League for the Independence of Vietnam (Viet Nam Doc Lap Dong Minh Hoi, or Vietminh). The goal of the Vietminh was to defeat the French and the Japanese. To defeat their enemies, the Vietminh planned to combine the nationalist movements in the cities with peasant rebellions in the rural areas. Ho and the Vietminh believed it was important to gain the support of the peasants to achieve the goal of Vietnamese independence.

In March 1945, the Japanese invaded Vietnam again. This time they revoked the 1883 treaty that established Vietnam as a French colony and declared Vietnam independent under Japanese protection. Ho and the Communists, however, considered Japan to be the main enemy and cooperated with the French to get rid of the Japanese.

Ho also worked with the United States, providing intelligence information about Japan's war efforts in Indochina. Ho helped rescue American pilots who had been shot down by the Japanese. He hoped that the United States would, in return, support his independence movement once the war was over.

After World War II, the Japanese were expelled from Vietnam. But Ho's struggle against the French continued. With France weakened by the world war, Ho and the Communists saw their chance. Within days of the Japanese surrender on August 15, 1945, the Vietnamese revolution began. The Vietminh soon controlled the northern part of the country. They announced the formation of a provisional, or temporary, government called the Democratic Republic of Vietnam (DRV), with Ho Chi Minh as its

Franco-Vietnamese medics treat a wounded Vietminh prisoner after a firefight south of Hanoi.

president and minister of foreign affairs. The Vietminh were not successful in defeating the French in the south, however. French troops seized control of the city of Saigon.

By March of 1946, the French were threatening to retake the northern part of the country from the Communists. Ho was able to negotiate a compromise in which France recognized the DRV. In return Ho and the Vietminh accepted a small French military presence in the north. The DRV also became a member of the French Union, an organization of France's colonial holdings around the world. Both sides agreed to let South Vietnamese citizens vote in national elections to decide who should lead South Vietnam, the French or the Vietminh.

In December 1946, France reversed its position and demanded that the Vietminh relinquish control of the north. The Vietminh instead attacked the French, and war broke out. The fighting continued for nearly a year and a half.

The United States Chooses Sides

It was during this period that the United States became involved in the conflict. Rather than support Ho Chi Minh, as Ho had hoped, the United States instead supported France, its longtime ally.

Vietnamese youths march through the streets of Saigon during Independence Day festivities in 1952.

After granting limited independence to Vietnam in 1948, French officials named former Vietnamese emperor Bao Dai to lead the new government.

In 1948, France offered a solution to the war in an attempt to prevent further fighting. On June 5, France granted independence to all of Vietnam in the form of associated statehood. France called the new government the State of Vietnam and appointed former Vietnamese emperor Bao Dai, who was pro-French, to lead it. The Vietminh were not satisfied with this solution. By setting up a pro-French government and not allowing a leader to be determined by election, the French were still controlling Vietnam.

To the United States, however, associated statehood seemed a step in the right direction. Although the United States supported the eventual establishment of an independent Vietnam, it did not want a Communist government there. To the United States, allowing France to keep its old colony was preferable to letting Vietnam fall to communism. On February 7, 1950, the United States officially recognized the State of Vietnam.

The fighting between the French and Vietnamese continued. With military aid from Communist China, Ho and the Vietminh concentrated on freeing the north, where the Communists were strongest.

The Communists concentrated on wearing down the French, hoping that the French would tire of the war. They knew that, in France, people were growing weary of the conflict. The Communists attacked the French military at its weakest points and kept the French forces thinned out by mounting attacks great distances apart. These guerrilla tactics, along with efforts to organize resistance to the French, were quite successful. By late 1952, the Vietminh had regained control of much of the north.

As the Communists hoped, the French were tiring of the war. They proposed to negotiate a diplomatic settlement, and the Vietnamese Communists agreed. But before the peace talks actually began, the Communists decided to attack and hold a French fortified camp to help give them leverage in the forthcoming talks.

On March 13, 1954, the Vietminh began the siege of Dien Bien Phu, a French-occupied town near the Laotian border. The siege ended with the surrender of the French on May 7, a few days after a peace conference on the Far East began in Geneva, Switzerland.

The Geneva conference was attended by other Eastern and Western nations with interests in the Far East. The United States was one of the Western nations that attended the conference.

Cease-Fire Splits Vietnam in Two

In July the conference produced two documents known as the Geneva Accords. The first was a cease-fire agreement signed by Vietnam and France. It created a demarcation, or boundary, line near the seventeenth parallel. The area around the line became

Members of the French Foreign Legion question a suspected Vietminh fighter found hiding in the jungle.

known as the Demilitarized Zone, or DMZ. The French regrouped south of that line and the Vietminh moved its forces north of the line.

This cease-fire formally divided Vietnam into two separate governments. The part of Vietnam north of the demarcation line was called the Democratic Republic of Vietnam (North Vietnam) and was led by Ho Chi Minh. The portion south of the line was called the Republic of Vietnam (South Vietnam). Ngo Dinh Diem, a nationalist who was anti-Communist and anti-French, was named president of South Vietnam.

A second agreement called for national elections to be held in July 1956. These elections would be supervised by an international commission. The demarcation line, the agreement said, "should not in any way be interpreted as constituting a political territory boundary." This meant that the boundary was intended to be only a temporary one.

Both the United States and the new government of South Vietnam refused to approve this agreement. Both governments knew that if free elections were held, the Communist Vietminh would surely win and take control of South Vietnam. The Communists would gain at the ballot box what they had previously been unable to win on the battlefield or at the negotiating table.

Vietminh Gen. Quang Buu (seated) signs the 1954 agreement bringing an end to fighting in Indochina. The agreement, reached during negotiations in Geneva, Switzerland, came to be known as the Geneva Accords.

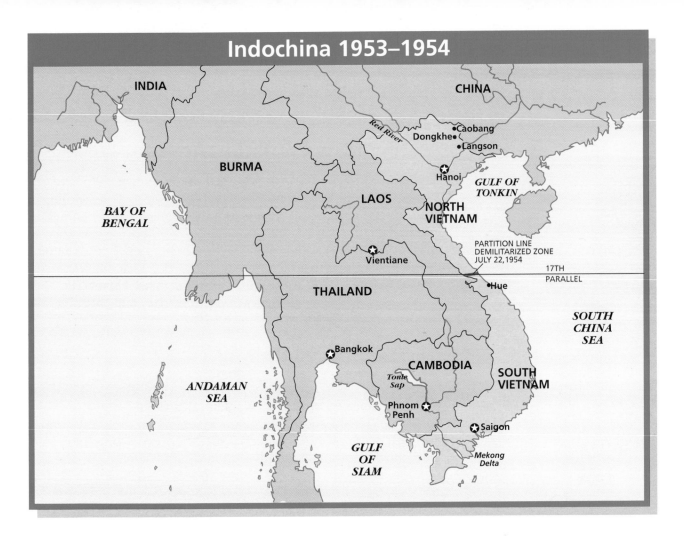

Indochina 1953–1954

U.S. Policy After Geneva

After the Geneva Accords of 1954, the United States' goal of containing communism in Vietnam remained the same. But with the French gone, the United States needed a new ally to assist in making sure South Vietnam did not fall. The United States aided Ngo Dinh Diem's government in exchange for his support of the United States. Together, Diem and the United States conspired to thwart the 1956 elections. Diem knew he was a certain loser to the more popular Vietminh if free elections were held.

In the years to follow, however, Diem proved to be a difficult ally and a poor leader. Diem was unable to build a stable government to replace that of the French. He ruled by intimidation and even murder. Popular land reforms established earlier by the Vietminh were overturned so that Diem and his family could gain more land. Diem's poor rule left the South Vietnamese economy in ruins. U.S. aid was the only thing keeping Diem's government and his policies in force.

Ngo Dinh Diem was named president of South Vietnam after Vietnam was split into separate north and south governments.

Though unhappy with Diem's leadership, the United States continued to support him through the 1950s and into the 1960s because he was pro-American. Diem's unpopularity weakened the United States' position in Vietnam. The Vietnamese people began to dislike the United States as much as they disliked Diem.

Communists Continue the Fight

The cancellation of the 1956 elections convinced Ho and the North Vietnamese Communists that military action would be required to reunite North and South Vietnam. Throughout the last half of the 1950s, the Communists worked to gain support among the people of South Vietnam. In 1960, the Vietminh changed its name to the Vietcong (VC). The Vietcong were successful in organizing the rural peasants against Diem. The Vietcong also used guerrilla tactics to terrorize and frustrate the South Vietnamese army.

Worsening Conditions

In the early 1960s, economic, political, and military conditions in South Vietnam continued to worsen. The United States responded with more aid and military personnel. When President John F. Kennedy took office in January 1961, there were only nine hundred official U.S. military advisers in South Vietnam. By the end

In his first two years in office, President John F. Kennedy expanded the number of U.S. military advisers in South Vietnam from about 900 to 11,000.

Three thousand people from the village of Kham Duc were relocated to this fortress village, one of many designed to separate South Vietnamese peasants from the Vietcong.

Helmeted rebel troops and Vietnamese civilians at the gates of the presidential palace in Saigon during the 1963 revolt against the regime of President Ngo Dinh Diem.

of 1962, the figure had reached eleven thousand. For the next six years, U.S. personnel would continue to be sent to South Vietnam in response to ever-worsening conditions.

The U.S. military strategy was to help the South Vietnamese fight the Vietcong. To accomplish this, the United States created a network of armed villages called strategic hamlets. South Vietnamese peasants were moved into the hamlets to keep them separated from the Vietcong. The United States hoped that this would prevent the peasants from helping the Vietcong. In a separate effort, U.S. Special Forces, or Green Berets, were sent into the central highlands to train tribespeople to support the United States against the Vietcong.

Neither of these two strategies successfully stopped the Vietcong. By mid-1963, the Vietcong were so well established in South Vietnam that President Kennedy faced a critical decision. Either he had to commit even more aid to Vietnam or withdraw altogether, which would surely result in a Communist victory. Kennedy did not want to let South Vietnam fall to the Communists. At the same time, election year was coming up, and he knew that increased aid or military action could hurt his chances at reelection.

The Domino Theory

The domino theory is the concept that if the United States allowed one government to fall to communism, others would surely follow. President Dwight Eisenhower first discussed the concept publicly in a press conference on April 7, 1954, when commenting on the strategic importance of Indochina to the free world:

> …finally, you have the broader considerations that might follow what you might call the "falling domino" principle.
>
> You had a row of dominoes set up, and you knocked over the first one, and what would happen to the last one was the certainty that it would go over very quickly. So you have the beginning of a disintegration that would have the most profound influences.

The domino theory was used to justify aid to the French between the end of World War II and their withdrawal from Vietnam in 1954. It was also used to justify support for the Diem government of South Vietnam between 1954 and 1963. President Lyndon Johnson used the domino theory to justify the expansion of U.S. military operations in South Vietnam after the Gulf of Tonkin incident in 1964.

Supporters of the domino theory argue that a Communist victory in any country lessens U.S. credibility with other small nations threatened by a Communist takeover. Critics discount the idea of a worldwide Communist revolution and

President Eisenhower was the first to verbalize the domino theory, which has become a cornerstone of U.S. foreign policy. Many presidents since Eisenhower, including Richard Nixon and Ronald Reagan, invoked the domino theory to justify U.S. involvement in other countries.

blame the unrest in areas such as Southeast Asia and Central America on conditions that already exist within each country.

Late in 1963, before Kennedy made any decision, two extraordinary events happened. On November 1, the unpopular Diem was killed in a successful coup, or revolt, against his government. The coup had been organized by Diem's own generals. Members of the U.S. State Department had known about the coup in advance and secretly had even pledged U.S. support for the generals. The State Department knew Diem stood in the way of achieving American goals in Vietnam.

Three weeks later on November 22, 1963, President Kennedy was assassinated in Dallas, Texas. Lyndon Johnson became president on the same day. In the hours immediately following Kennedy's death, Johnson wondered if Kennedy had been killed in retaliation for U.S. support of the coup against Diem. But no evidence has ever been found to connect the two deaths.

Johnson inherited the critical decision that Kennedy had not lived to make. Should the United States increase its commitment to Vietnam or withdraw? Like Kennedy, Johnson found it to be a difficult decision that was tied to his hopes for reelection. He hoped to put the decision off until after the election, but an incident in the summer of 1964 helped make the decision for him.

Rebel troops attack the presidential palace with heavy machine guns. The revolt led to the collapse of the Diem government.

The Gulf of Tonkin Controversy

Controversy surrounds the Gulf of Tonkin incident. Some critics of the Vietnam War claim that the version of the events Lyndon B. Johnson gave to the public was untrue. They claim that American ships had been sent to the Gulf of Tonkin deliberately to provoke the North Vietnamese into attacking them. They also claim that in the second incident on August 4, American ships were not actually attacked, they were only threatened.

The Gulf of Tonkin incident, critics charge, was fabricated to give President Johnson the excuse he needed to get Congress to support increased U.S. involvement in the war in South Vietnam.

To support their argument, critics charge that the Gulf of Tonkin Resolution passed by Congress was actually written as much as two months before the incidents that occurred on August 2 and 4. If that is true, it means that President Johnson was planning to increase U.S. involvement in Vietnam long before the attacks occurred rather than in reaction to them. It also means that Johnson lied to America during his campaign for reelection. During his campaign, he had cautioned against further U.S. military involvement in Vietnam.

The complete truth about the Gulf of Tonkin incident may never be known. It is a fact, however, that the incident marked the

Did Johnson deliberately send troops into the Gulf of Tonkin to provoke a North Vietnamese attack?

beginning of the United States' direct military involvement in Vietnam. The conflicting stories over what really happened have left the American entry into the Vietnam War clouded in mystery.

The North Vietnamese attack on the U.S. Navy destroyer Maddox *enraged President Lyndon Johnson.*

The Gulf of Tonkin Incident

On August 2, 1964, the U.S. destroyer *Maddox,* while on a surveillance mission in the Gulf of Tonkin off the North Vietnamese coast, was attacked by three North Vietnamese patrol boats. The attack was easily repelled. Two days later, North Vietnamese patrol boats again attacked the *Maddox* and a second destroyer, the USS *Turner Joy.* Neither ship was damaged, but the idea that the Vietnamese would directly attack U.S. ships enraged Johnson. That same day Johnson ordered retaliatory air strikes against North Vietnamese air bases and oil storage depots. U.S. planes flew sixty missions and sank or damaged thirty North Vietnamese boats.

Johnson then went before Congress and requested authority to defend American forces in Southeast Asia. The two attacks, along with reports that the North Vietnamese army was massing near the seventeenth parallel for a possible invasion of the South, created a sense of urgency in Congress.

In response to Johnson's request, Congress passed the Gulf of Tonkin Resolution on August 7. The resolution stated that "Congress approves and supports the determination of the President, as Commander in Chief, to take all necessary measures

A second attack on the Maddox *and an attack on another U.S. Navy destroyer,* Turner Joy, *(above) prompted Johnson to order retaliatory air strikes against the North Vietnamese.*

Lt. Keith Bane, gunnery officer on the Maddox, *kneels near a machine-gun hole made during the North Vietnamese attack on the destroyer in 1964.*

to repel any armed attack against the forces of the United States and to prevent further aggression." Members of Congress were almost unanimous in their support for the president.

While the U.S. goal of containing the spread of communism in Vietnam remained the same, the Gulf of Tonkin Resolution signaled a significant change. To keep South Vietnam from toppling, the United States would try and do what the French government had not done and what the South Vietnamese government under Diem had not done. The United States would defend South Vietnam against communism. The escalation of U.S. military efforts in South Vietnam was about to begin.

CHAPTER TWO

The United States Escalates the War

President Johnson used the authority given to him by the Gulf of Tonkin Resolution to expand, or escalate, U.S. involvement in Vietnam. For the United States, that meant sending combat soldiers to fight with the South Vietnamese against the Communist forces of the Vietcong and North Vietnamese army.

Johnson hoped that by sending U.S. forces to help, he could keep North Vietnam from quickly defeating South Vietnam. The South Vietnamese government and army were weak from years of fighting. Johnson believed sending U.S. troops would give the South Vietnamese time to strengthen their government and armed forces. Then the South Vietnamese could resume the fighting on their own. By preventing defeat, Johnson believed he was accomplishing his goal of containing communism.

When escalating U.S. involvement, President Johnson and his advisers made certain decisions that would shape America's entire war effort. First the president believed that the United States should fight a limited war, or a war that was kept primarily within the borders of South Vietnam. Although he considered invading North Vietnam, Johnson decided against it. Invading North Vietnam might have caused its allies, China and the Soviet Union, to join the war. Johnson feared that war with China and the Soviet Union could destroy the world. Both of these countries were already aiding North Vietnam with arms and supplies. Johnson believed a limited war would not further antagonize either country.

President Johnson decided to send U.S. combat soldiers to join South Vietnamese soldiers against the Communist forces of the Vietcong and North Vietnamese army.

The decision to fight a limited war might have been a good political decision, but it would prove to be a poor military one. By not invading North Vietnam, the Communists could never really be defeated, which meant they could keep up the fight in South Vietnam.

Limiting the war to South Vietnam created another disadvantage for the United States. China and the Soviet Union shipped supplies to the North Vietnamese Communists along the Ho Chi Minh Trail. This trail went through the countries of Laos and Cambodia. The decision to keep the war limited to South Vietnam meant that the United States could not seal off the Ho Chi Minh Trail and stop the flow of arms and supplies to the Communists fighting in South Vietnam. If the trail could have been closed, the Communists would have had far fewer supplies. That might have made the war end sooner. As it was, Communist forces in South Vietnam remained well supplied.

The United States' plan was to fight a war of attrition. This meant that U.S. soldiers would help destroy Communist soldiers, supplies, and war-related factories. Ideally, Communist forces would be so busy rebuilding that they would be unable to fight. That would give South Vietnam the time it needed to strengthen its government and improve its armed forces.

The Ho Chi Minh Trail

North Vietnam shipped weapons, supplies, and soldiers to the revolutionary Vietcong soldiers fighting in South Vietnam. For many years, much of these materials were shipped south along a route known as the Ho Chi Minh Trail. The route was named in honor of North Vietnam's revolutionary hero.

The Ho Chi Minh Trail extended from North Vietnam through the neighboring country of Laos, then wound its way south through the country of Cambodia before entering South Vietnam from the west. The route was roundabout for a very good reason. By locating this supply route outside of North and South Vietnam in more neutral territory, the Communists had a better chance of getting their supplies far to the south where they were needed.

The United States knew about the Ho Chi Minh Trail. Closing down the trail, however, meant risking expansion of the Vietnam War into Laos and Cambodia. In the early years of the war, the United States was reluctant to do this, and the supplies poured into South Vietnam. Eventually, the United States dropped bombs on the Ho Chi Minh Trail to prevent supplies from reaching South Vietnam. But the bombs never closed the trail completely. The Communists were able to repair whatever damage the bombs did and keep the route open. The Ho Chi Minh Trail played a large role in the Communists' eventual victory in Vietnam.

Peasants and others walked various routes, including the Ho Chi Minh Trail, carrying supplies on their backs for Vietcong soldiers fighting in the south.

President Johnson and Vietnam

Lyndon Baines Johnson became the thirty-sixth president of the United States on November 22, 1963, the day President Kennedy was assassinated. The new president immediately faced the decision of what to do in Vietnam. During his reelection campaign in 1964, Johnson warned against increasing American involvement in Vietnam. His stand as a peace candidate helped him win reelection. In 1965, President Johnson reversed this position, ordered bombing in North Vietnam, and sent American troops into battle.

The President also dreamed of building a Great Society in America. He declared "unconditional war" on poverty. With his leadership, Congress passed laws that helped pay health care costs for senior citizens, made it easier for black people to vote, helped the unemployed, expanded the food stamp program for the needy, and made it easier for young people to get jobs. Never had the country seen so much legislation that favored the common citizen.

But President Johnson's Great Society was shattered by the Vietnam War. The president was inexperienced in international affairs. His decision to escalate the war would prove to be a costly mistake for the country and for himself. Although he insisted that the country could afford both the war and the Great Society programs he wanted, his critics claimed that America could not pay for both "guns" and "butter." They were right. His failure to bring a successful resolution to the Vietnam War caused much turmoil in the country and forced cutbacks in the social programs he helped create. His popularity fell, and in 1968, he announced he

President Johnson's dream of building a Great Society in the United States was shattered by his decision to escalate American involvement in the Vietnam War.

would not run for reelection. He is remembered more as a war president than the creator of the Great Society. President Johnson died on January 22, 1973, five days before the peace treaty was signed that ended America's involvement in Vietnam.

This huge Sky Crane CH-54A U.S. Army helicopter carried enormous loads of supplies and heavy equipment between bases and the battlefield.

The United States had a large military and vast natural resources with which to escalate its involvement in the war. U.S. armies were what Gen. John W. Vessey called "top notch." In addition, the United States had developed an extensive arsenal of high-technology weapons. Its most potent weapon was its air power. With various planes and bombers, the United States could bomb targets anywhere. It could launch air strikes against military bases, supply depots, and factories far away from the fighting. During battle, planes could support American soldiers fighting on the ground by bombing enemy troops.

Another important piece of American technology was the helicopter. By the 1960s, the United States had helicopters that were capable of carrying large numbers of troops and heavy equipment. By using helicopters, the Americans could create instant supply lines between bases and the battlefield.

The U.S. armies were skilled practitioners of traditional warfare—direct combat between two warring factions. In direct combat, the side with the best soldiers, the best training, the best equipment, and the best generals conquers the land and wins the war. Traditional warfare was the only kind of war the United States knew how to fight.

But in Vietnam, the United States quickly discovered that it was seldom able to fight a traditional war. First, the decision to fight a limited war prevented the U.S. army from conquering North Vietnam, which would have been the probable result of a traditional war. But even more important, the Communists' method of warfare prevented the United States from fighting the war in the style with which it was most familiar.

What U.S. Troops Encountered in Vietnam

When the first American combat soldiers landed in Vietnam in March 1965, it seemed like the biblical giant Goliath had crossed the Pacific Ocean to battle David. Compared to the United States, North Vietnam was indeed like David, small and powerless. But, like David, the North Vietnamese would prove to be very resourceful. They would prove to be unlike any enemy the United States had ever faced.

The Communists avoided the direct combat that the Americans favored. Instead, they launched surprise attacks, or ambushes, upon the American and South Vietnamese armies and then quickly slipped away to hide in the jungle or in the miles of tunnels that honeycombed the hills. The Communists moved quickly

Soldiers of the U.S. Ninth Infantry Division wade through muddy, waist-deep water while on patrol in South Vietnam in 1968.

A U.S. soldier carefully picks his way through a muddy stream lined with sharp-tipped pungi stakes (left). A medic treats a soldier wounded by an exploding white phosphorus booby trap (right).

through the familiar jungle terrain, shooting at their enemy many times from different places. With shots coming from so many locations, the Americans often believed the Communists' numbers were much higher than they actually were. Such tactics confused and harassed the Americans. They kept U.S. soldiers on the lookout for attack rather than allowing them to pursue their own tactics.

The North Vietnamese, even after they had slipped away to hide, used inventive weapons to harass and confuse the Americans. They created booby traps by rigging concealed grenades or land mines to trip wires. When a soldier's foot tripped the wire, it set off the explosive, killing or seriously injuring him. The Communists dug pits and filled them with land mines, covering the pits with leaves so that they looked like solid ground. When a soldier stepped or fell into the pit, the land mine exploded. Other pits were lined with sharpened sticks of bamboo called *pungi* stakes that cut human flesh like knives. Thorny branches were bent back and attached to trip wires. When triggered, the branches would sweep into the faces of soldiers. Such weapons made the Americans even less effective in the unfamiliar jungle, giving the Communists a distinct advantage.

A Vietnamese child, whose body is covered with burns from a napalm bomb, was one of many innocent victims of the war.

The guerrilla warfare tactics would prove to be far more suitable to the mountainous terrain and dense jungles than the technological weapons the United States used. To offset them, the Americans used chemical herbicides to make trees and bushes drop their leaves and make the enemy more visible. The most well-known chemical was Agent Orange. Napalm, a sticky substance that burned like gasoline, was also used. It was dropped on the landscape and then ignited, turning the countryside into an inferno that destroyed everything in its path.

Napalm and Agent Orange were destructive not only to the enemy, but also to civilians, friendly troops, and the countryside itself. These weapons would become very controversial during the war as their destructiveness became known to the world.

In addition to the military advantage given them by their guerrilla warfare tactics, the North Vietnamese also had the advantage of a more defined goal than the United States. The North Vietnamese had already been fighting for over twenty years to defeat the South Vietnamese government and reunify North and South Vietnam. Even many South Vietnamese supported and worked toward this goal. Since North Vietnam's

Aerial photographs show a lush South Vietnamese mangrove forest before (upper left) and after (lower left) it was destroyed by herbicides in 1965. A close-up view (right) shows the scarred, leafless trees that resulted from heavy bombing.

Tunnel Warfare

The Communist troops built tunnels to hide in and to store their supplies. These tunnels were many layers deep and stretched for miles below the Vietnamese countryside. In order to fight the North Vietnamese, U.S. soldiers often had to attempt to search and destroy these tunnels in tunnel warfare.

Tunnel warfare became one of the most unpopular tasks American soldiers faced. When a tunnel was found, smoke grenades were thrown in to reveal other entrances to the tunnel. Frequently tear gas grenades were thrown into the tunnel to harass enemy soldiers and drive them outside or down into the lower levels. When all was quiet, a soldier known as a tunnel rat donned a gas mask and a bulletproof garment called a flak jacket. He entered the tunnel and slowly worked his way through it searching for the enemy and their supplies. When the job was finished, the soldiers would blow up or bulldoze the tunnel entrances so the enemy could not use the tunnels again. Tunnel warfare was dangerous and hard on the nerves. The enemy could leap out of the darkness at any moment. U.S. soldiers sometimes skipped searching the tunnel and simply blew up or bulldozed the entrances, trapping the enemy soldiers inside.

Since the tunnel systems were so long, it was impossible to be sure every entrance was destroyed. Often the enemy returned and with a little work, reopened the tunnel for use.

An American soldier inspects a Vietcong tunnel. Many of these tunnels were well fortified and well stocked.

goal was a clear military one, victory was easier to measure—North Vietnam knew they had won when they defeated South Vietnam. America's goal, however, was to keep South Vietnam from falling, not to invade or defeat North Vietnam. Thus victory was harder to determine.

Finally, the North Vietnamese had devised a plan to wear down the United States' resolve. The North Vietnamese were prepared to fight a very long war. They hoped to wear down the United States so that Americans back home would tire of the war and pressure the U.S. government to withdraw. A decade earlier, the Communists had used that strategy to defeat the French.

A Pattern to the War

The differences in the goals and methods of the United States and North Vietnam caused battles between them to follow a very predictable pattern. The Communists made many small attacks, inflicting whatever casualties they could before slipping away. In a single week in July 1965, for example, *Time* magazine reported that the Communists had attacked South Vietnamese or American forces in nine different locations throughout South Vietnam.

Helicopters enabled the U.S. military to drop soldiers into the heart of battle. Here, soldiers dodge enemy fire as they leave a helicopter.

But, when a more traditional battle occurred, it was the better-equipped Americans who always won. In a battle in the Ia Drang River Valley in November 1965, for example, fewer than five hundred Americans defeated more than three thousand North Vietnamese. The Americans used helicopters to create instant supply lines and moved troops and artillery into better positions as the battlefield shifted. They used bombers to destroy or weaken enemy positions. These high-technology weapons more than compensated for the fact that the Americans were far outnumbered.

Mines and bombs killed and injured many civilians. At left, a young woman mourns a death caused by an exploding mine. At right, a youth wounded in a bomb blast awaits treatment in a Saigon hospital.

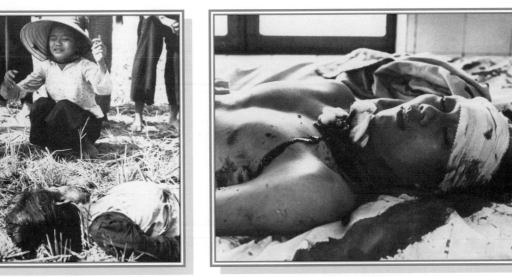

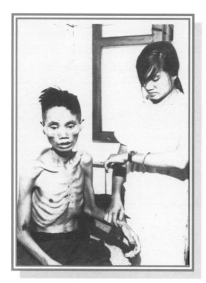

The Communists recruited many villagers, but also suffered defections. This defector, recaptured by the Vietcong, was deliberately starved in a prison camp.

Unfortunately, the battles and guerrilla attacks always seemed to result in a stalemate. U.S. forces would drive the North Vietnamese out of one area, only to have them return to other areas. U.S. soldiers were never able to see a clear progression in the battles with the North Vietnamese.

Although they had suffered very high casualties, the Communists were able to replace their losses with new troops recruited from both North and South Vietnam. The Communists returned to the villages and countryside after the American and South Vietnamese forces secured them and left. Plus, the Communists had the support of many of the South Vietnamese peasants, who allowed them to hide in their homes when necessary. All of these elements offset the battle victories that the United States had scored.

This lack of progression led Gen. William Westmoreland, the military commander in charge of U.S. troops in Vietnam, to recommend sending more U.S. soldiers to Vietnam. Almost every month, General Westmoreland requested more troops from Washington. If the United States did not commit more men to Vietnam, the general argued, the war would be lost, and South Vietnam would fall to the Communists. By the end of 1965, there were over 170,000 U.S. troops in South Vietnam. America's political and military leaders hoped that more troops, more bombs, and more fighting would lead to victory.

By the end of 1965 there were over 170,000 U.S. troops in South Vietnam.

A Grunt's Life

Foot soldiers in Vietnam were nicknamed grunts, for it was they who did the everyday, or grunt, work. In December of 1966, eighteen-year-old marine private Jim Mason arrived in Vietnam. "I felt I was fulfilling an obligation to my country," he recalled years later, "and I had an opportunity to see what war was like. I remember telling my English teacher back in the spring that I wanted to see what war was like."

Private first class Mason soon found out. Two weeks after his arrival, his unit was sent out into the field, or "in country" as the soldiers called it. He was sent to a base camp near the Demilitarized Zone (DMZ), the neutral area along the border between North and South Vietnam. That very night, he went out on his first patrol:

> It was the middle of January, rainy and cold. We set up in the rain. I remember the rain drops made such a loud noise on my poncho, like drumbeats. I was excited and scared at the same time. Just being out there at night was scary. We were sitting in some pineapple bushes, and I saw movement. I nudged the guy next to me and whispered that I had seen something move. He whispered back, "Don't shoot. They leave us alone at night and we leave them alone." That was my first encounter with the enemy.

There would be many such encounters with the enemy—and some with actual fighting—as Mason's life in country settled into a new routine. He went out on patrol for about four hours almost every night. There were other patrols during the day. When not on patrol, his unit went about other duties. They went to the river to get drinking water and to wash the clothes they were wearing. The supply truck came, bringing mail, food, clothing, ammunition, and replacement soldiers. While in country, Mason ate cold C-rations out of cans—spaghetti and meatballs or beans and franks, sometimes fruit. And there were crackers and cheese, always crackers and cheese. When there was no work to do, he often played cards with other soldiers to help pass the time and relieve the boredom. During a twenty-four-hour period, if he was lucky, Mason could get about eight hours of sleep—three or four hours at night and catnaps during the day. Often, Mason thought about how different being in country was from anything he had ever known. "I was away from home, away from the service routine that I knew, and the war was completely new to me."

Mason felt "a routine sense of danger" that made his shoulders tighten with tension. He was always on the alert—watching for movements in the night, listening for the snap of a twig or some other warning of his next encounter with an enemy he would rarely see. Frustration, tension, and the boredom of waiting to do his job were his constant companions.

Foot soldiers nearly always felt a sense of danger in the field.

General Westmoreland (left) visits U.S. Army headquarters northeast of Saigon.

With guns cocked, U.S. Marines question a suspected Vietcong sympathizer, one of many captured during a sweep near Da Nang.

American troops began to take over more of the fighting from the South Vietnamese. At the end of 1966, 320,000 Americans were serving in combat and support roles in Vietnam. More than 6,400 Americans had been killed. By September of 1967, U.S. troops serving in Vietnam had increased to 464,000. In October, American casualties passed the 13,000 mark.

A Military Stalemate

Late in 1967, General Westmoreland met privately with President Johnson and delivered disturbing news. He told him that despite the fact that enemy casualties were far higher than American casualties and that the United States had won every major battle, the war had reached a stalemate. Westmoreland concluded that even if thousands of additional troops were sent to Vietnam, the war could drag on another three years.

"At the end of 1967," historian Gabriel Kolko wrote, "it was becoming increasingly obvious that the [North Vietnamese soldiers'] ability to adapt to each U.S. escalation had created a military stalemate.

In a sense, this stalemate had existed from the very point that the United States had escalated its involvement in the war in 1965. The United States knew only one way to fight a war—with high-technology weapons and large armies. Whenever the United States determined that something more had to be done to prevent South Vietnam from losing, it simply did more of what it was already doing, using more soldiers, bombs, and fighting, hoping to turn the war around.

Even when it became obvious that this strategy was not working, the Americans could not afford to discontinue their war efforts and take time to rethink their tactics. To stop fighting would surely allow the Communists to win. If the Communists were ever to be defeated, Johnson and his advisers had little choice but to keep the stalemate going while they decided what else to do.

U.S. military forces were becoming demoralized and confused. They had been taught to fight and to win. But victory seemed a long way off. Their military leaders did not seem to want them to win. American soldiers were no longer sure why they were in Vietnam or what they were fighting for.

On Christmas Day 1967, U.S. Marine Jim Mason's tour of duty ended, and he left Vietnam for the United States. "I felt no sense of accomplishment other than my friends and I had helped each other to survive. We didn't act to help our country, but to save our buddies." His frustrations were shared by many American soldiers serving in Vietnam.

The Tet Offensive

What was a bad military situation for the United States was a good one for the Communists. Vo Nguyen Giap, the commander of the Communist forces, sensed that the time was right for a major military attack. Giap began preparing for the attack in the early days of 1968 by moving troops and supplies into positions throughout South Vietnam.

On January 21, the Communists attacked the American base and airplane runway of Khe Sanh near the DMZ, the neutral area along the border between North and South Vietnam. Khe Sanh was an important base to the Americans. From there, U.S. forces could monitor enemy activity along the DMZ and the Ho Chi Minh Trail in Laos.

The Communists were soon beaten back by American forces. The Communists then followed the attack with a barrage of artillery fire that damaged the runway, destroyed the main ammunition stores, and damaged some aircraft. They built a network of positions around the base and renewed their attack upon Khe Sanh and American positions in surrounding areas.

As weather conditions allowed, the Americans retaliated with air strikes that hammered Communist positions. The Americans also began to airlift replacement munitions and supplies into the base. U.S. air and artillery power prevented the base from falling

In early 1968, Gen. Vo Nguyen Giap, commander of the Communist forces, sensed that the time was right for a major military attack.

Hearts and Minds

While warfare raged in the jungles and fields of South Vietnam, another kind of battle raged throughout the country—the battle to win the support of the South Vietnamese peasants. It became known as the battle for "hearts and minds."

The Americans knew that the Communists depended on peasant cooperation. Peasants gave the Communists information about the enemy, shared food and other supplies, and provided them a place to hide when the enemy was near. To the peasants, the Communists represented an alternative to the unpopular South Vietnamese government. Between 1954 and his death in 1963, the South Vietnamese leader Ngo Dinh Diem had turned the peasants against his government through oppressive rule and unfair land reform programs. The government of his eventual successor, Nguyen Van Thieu, was just as unpopular.

South Vietnamese troops urge villagers, who often sheltered the Vietcong, to flee the scene of fighting that left several Vietcong dead.

Although many South Vietnamese peasants supported the Communists over the Americans, others—including this farmer—fled their homes to escape the Vietcong.

The Americans themselves were often automatically disliked by many peasants because they supported the South Vietnamese government. American-dropped bombs also destroyed villages and farms, making it hard for the peasants to grow enough food to survive.

Because the Americans were unsuccessful in building support among the peasants, they were also unsuccessful in eliminating support for the Communists. The United States created a special program called Operation Phoenix to seek out the people who supported the enemy in the rural areas and eliminate that support. Too often, eliminating Communist supporters simply meant killing them. An estimated twenty thousand suspected enemy supporters were killed during Operation Phoenix. But the program alienated far more peasants than it eliminated potential enemies.

The Communists had programs of their own that eliminated anyone suspected of aiding the Americans and the South Vietnamese government. They often terrorized the peasants into supporting them with threats and brutal beatings. Thousands of peasants were killed by the Communists as well. The peasants were caught in the middle between both sides. As the war progressed, they suffered terribly.

Vietnamese peasants were often caught in the middle of hostilities. At left, a three-year-old child wounded in a Vietcong attack. Below, a Vietnamese family is forced to relocate.

A platoon of soldiers struggles through high elephant grass to reach the American base at Khe Sanh, which came under attack in 1968.

into Communist hands. The Communists launched attacks on February 17, 18, and 29 that were driven back with U.S. bombs, rockets, and artillery.

But the siege of Khe Sanh was not Giap's main offensive target, as Americans had first thought. In fact it may only have been a diversion. Ten days after the first attack on Khe Sanh, the Communists launched surprise attacks on major cities in South Vietnam and most American bases and airfields.

The attacks began at dawn on January 30, 1968, the first day of Tet, the traditional Vietnamese new year. In previous years of the war, Tet had been a time of truce. Because American attention was focused on the developing battle at Khe Sanh, Giap and the Communists managed to take South Vietnam by surprise.

Fierce Fighting

Most of the attacks were beaten back within hours, but others were repelled only after days or weeks of fierce fighting. In the capital city of Saigon, for example, nineteen Vietcong commandos attacked the American Embassy. Two American guards were killed at the beginning of the attack. Other guards held

U.S. Marines take cover behind a tank during the 1968 Tet Offensive. The surprise Communist attacks led to bitter fighting, many wounded, and many dead.

off the commandos until more soldiers and supplies could be helicoptered in. By midmorning, all the commandos had been killed, and the embassy was secured again. Five Americans had been killed. At home, Americans were shocked and outraged by the attack on what they felt was American soil.

Elsewhere in Saigon, the Communists attacked the South Vietnamese presidential palace, a local radio station, and the headquarters of the South Vietnamese army. Seven hundred Communists attacked U.S. commander Westmoreland's compound at the American air base at nearby Tan Son Nhut. The fighting became so intense that Westmoreland ordered his personal staff to find weapons and join in defending the compound. Before the battle was over and the Communists retreated, twenty-three Americans were killed and eighty-five were wounded. Fifteen aircraft had been damaged.

South Vietnamese president Nguyen Van Thieu, Diem's successor, declared martial, or military, law in Saigon on the first day of the attack. It took a week to secure the city again. During heavy fighting in the streets, sections of Saigon were reduced to

Two American soldiers lie dead as three others watch for further movement from Vietcong commandos who attacked the U.S. Embassy in Saigon.

rubble. The fighting subsided by February 5 as the North Vietnamese army and Vietcong were driven out of the city.

Far to the north of Saigon, the city of Hue was also attacked and overrun on the morning of January 31. One of the Communists' main targets was the Citadel, an ancient palace whose grounds covered about two square miles. The Communists raised a Vietcong flag there on the first morning. Elsewhere in the city, Communists freed thousands of people who had been imprisoned by the South Vietnamese government. They also rounded up thousands of Catholics and South Vietnamese government officials. Many were shot because they were considered enemies of the state. Most of the rest simply vanished.

American marines and the South Vietnamese army drove into Hue, advancing block by block in bitter fighting. The Citadel was recaptured February 23, and the enemy forces retreated.

Collectively, these battles became known as the Tet Offensive. The offensive subsided by April 1968. Once again, the United States had won the battles, but the real victory went to the Communists.

The Tet Offensive made the United States realize that it had vastly underestimated its enemy. U.S. government and military leaders were taken almost by complete surprise at the size and force of the Tet Offensive. The offensive convinced an increasing number of America's political and military leaders that U.S. involvement would cost thousands of American lives and would produce nothing more than a stalemate.

An End to Escalation

In late February of 1968, a gloomy report from America's military headquarters in Vietnam demanded over 100,000 additional men. President Johnson asked his new secretary of defense, Clark Clifford, to review the American position in Vietnam before he made any decision on the request. Secretary of Defense Clifford concluded that 100,000 additional troops would not make enough difference to win in Vietnam. The president consulted his closest advisers, a group nicknamed "The Wise Old Men." He found that they, too, had turned against the war.

In the end Johnson refused to send the additional men. His refusal signaled the end of America's escalation of the Vietnam War.

South Vietnamese Chairman Nguyen Van Thieu (left), U.S. President Lyndon Johnson (center), and South Vietnamese Prime Minister Nguyen Cau Ky salute during the playing of national anthems at a 1967 meeting.

A young woman mourns her missing husband (top) during a funeral service held for hundreds of people massacred by the Vietcong during the Tet Offensive. U.S. Secretary of Defense Clark Clifford (above) concluded in 1968 that additional troops would not lead to an American victory in Vietnam.

After a battle, weary American marines rest in a ditch behind a wall of the Citadel, one of the main targets of the Communists during the Tet Offensive.

Under heavy guard, a young Vietcong fighter awaits interrogation after being captured during the Tet Offensive.

What the United States would do next was influenced only partly by the failures on the battlefield. At home, the war had divided and changed America. From 1965 to 1968, politicians, mothers, fathers, sisters, and brothers had escalated a war of their own on America's college campuses, streets, and in government buildings. It was a war against the Vietnam War.

President Johnson's next steps would have to end two wars. He would have to find a new way to bring peace to Vietnam. In doing so, he also would have to find a way that would bring peace to America as well.

CHAPTER THREE

The United States Protests the Vietnam War

I n 1963, singer Bob Dylan sang, "The times, they are a-changin'." These words more than any others best describe what happened in America during the 1960s. Social movements that had begun in the 1950s collided with historical events of the 1960s and brought stunning changes to America.

The election of forty-five-year-old John F. Kennedy to the presidency in 1960 marked the emergence of a new, vibrant leader for the new decade. In striking contrast to the grandfatherly Eisenhower of the 1950s, Kennedy symbolized change rather than status quo. "Ask not what your country can do for you, ask what you can do for your country," Kennedy challenged America in his inaugural address in January 1961. His challenge especially inspired young people to get involved in their country.

Less than three years later, however, Kennedy was felled by an assassin's bullet in Dallas, Texas. His untimely death cast a dark shadow over the rest of the decade and completed the 1960s' formula for change in America: Question everything, demand change, and, if necessary, resort to violence to make it happen.

In the sixties, most young men and women questioned the Establishment—the values, traditions, and views of their parents. Many rejected it and became hippies, dropping out of society to live together in communes. "Make love, not war," they demanded, and "Never trust anyone over thirty." For the first time in society, drug use became widespread and young people experimented with new freedoms.

The sexual revolution began in the sixties. The old sexual mores of marriage and family that had shaped American life for decades were challenged by a flood of books, movies, records, and plays that broke artistic and social rules. Premarital sex, interracial relationships, and pursuing one's "own thing" were glamorously portrayed in the media. American life imitated art. A new, more liberated culture emerged that rejected marriage, family, and traditional sexual relationships.

The civil rights movement that began in the fifties came of age during the sixties. Blacks and other minority groups demanded the same rights enjoyed by whites. Their demands led to violent confrontations between white people and black people. Race riots broke out in many American cities. Black leaders Malcolm X and the Rev. Martin Luther King Jr. were both assassinated during the sixties.

As the decade progressed, many Americans began to question the integrity and honesty of their government and its leaders. Such thinking would have been considered treason a decade earlier.

Every night, Americans sat down in their living rooms and saw the radical changes that were occurring across the country on their television sets. Television had been born in the forties

The Rev. Martin Luther King Jr. (left) and Malcolm X (right) were photographed together at this 1964 meeting. Within a few years, both would be dead from assassins' bullets.

Out of the Bedroom

"Leave it to Beaver" was one of the most popular television shows of the late 1950s. The show reflected and influenced American middle-class life, especially in the way it dealt with sexual mores of the times. The studio set where the show was filmed did not even include a bedroom for Beaver's parents, Ward and June. In America in the 1950s, sex was a taboo subject, in keeping with mores that had ruled society since the founding of the country.

The sixties exploded America's puritan attitudes about sex and brought it out of the bedroom. Permarital sex and cohabitation before marriage became part of American culture. Subjects like homosexuality were discussed openly in public for the first time. But along with new freedoms came new problems. Teenage pregnancies and sexually transmitted diseases began to increase dramatically in the sixties.

Nothing demonstrated that times had changed in America more than the arrival of the musical *Hair* on Broadway in 1968. Subtitled *An American Tribal Love-Rock Musical, Hair* celebrated all of the new freedoms the country was experimenting with throughout the sixties. It was antiestablishment, antiwar, prodrugs, prolove, and prosex. To celebrate America's new sexual freedom, the actors stripped off their clothes while singing the closing song of the first act. They stood stark naked before the theater audience, a sharp contrast to the early part of the decade when television would not even show a bedroom.

The musical, Hair*, shocked people across America with its final scene. In it, cast members stood before the audience naked.*

America Turns On

In the 1950s when people discussed drug abuse, they were mainly concerned about alcohol and cigarettes. The use of harder drugs was limited to the nation's ghettos, and many of the illegal drugs found on today's streets did not even exist then.

But during the 1960s, America turned on to drugs. By the end of the decade, drug abuse was no longer a minority problem tucked away in the ghetto, but a nationwide epidemic that threatened affluent white society.

America was in an experimental mood in the 1960s. To "expand their consciousnesses," people experimented with drugs like marijuana and LSD. The media, eager to document the growing counterculture in America, may have also helped popularize drug use by focusing on it.

Among young people, drug use went hand in hand with rock and roll and the sexual revolution. Young people saw sex, drugs, and rock and roll as entertaining and rebellious. Drugs were glorified in rock-and-roll songs. In the 1967 song "White Rabbit," for example, the band Jefferson Airplane advised young people to "feed your head" with drugs.

The drug issue helped widen the generation gap between parents and children. Parents condemned their children for taking drugs. Their children, on the other hand, pointed to their parents' use of alcohol and tobacco and labeled them hypocrites.

What may have started out as a fad became a national problem as more and more people turned to drug use as a form of escape from problems ranging from poverty to feelings of alienation and hopelessness.

Hippies relax on a boat, smoking a mixture of hashish and tobacco.

Vietnam soldiers also fed America's drug problem. Drugs were inexpensive and easily available in Asia, and many soldiers brought them back home and continued to use them. Others claim that soldiers learned about drugs at home first and continued to use them once in Vietnam. Whichever is true, troops in Vietnam often used drugs to escape the boredom and terror of jungle warfare.

and grew up in the fifties. But in the sixties, television matured and became the major news source for the country. Television cameras went anywhere and everywhere in America. Within hours of a major event, Americans saw pictures of it in their living rooms. Whether it was a civil rights march, a trip into outer space, the first U.S. appearance of the Beatles, or the funeral of an assassinated leader, television showed it all.

In the mid-sixties the Vietnam War became one more thing for Americans to question. Although the war was not the direct cause of all the unhappiness and unrest of the sixties, it touched nearly every other social movement in the country and seemed to attract bad feelings the way a magnet collects tacks and paper clips. Perhaps more than any other event of the sixties, the Vietnam War became a target for Americans to express their frustration and rage over many things that were going on at the time.

Vietnam Divides America

Vietnam divided America from the time it first became a major issue in 1964. The division was so tangible that the media used nicknames for those who were for or against the war. People who supported U.S. involvement in Vietnam were called hawks, and those opposed to U.S. involvement were called doves. Both hawks and doves maintained that they were right about Vietnam. Between 1964 and early 1968, the debate over what was right and wrong about U.S. involvement in Vietnam would nearly tear the country apart. It would force the majority of Americans, whose views on Vietnam were fairly neutral at the beginning of the war, to make a decision and take a stand. Many Americans would turn against the war, and early in 1968, the antiwar movement would heavily influence President Johnson's Vietnam policies.

In 1965, however, most Americans supported the war. Although they might not have favored increasing U.S. involvement, they trusted Johnson and his advisers to make the right decisions about what should be done. Since Johnson favored escalating U.S. involvement in Vietnam, this meant that, indirectly, these Americans supported the war because they supported the government.

However, when Johnson began to increase U.S. involvement in Vietnam, his action drew immediate criticism from a small portion of Americans, the doves. They protested Johnson's actions on both moral and strategic grounds. Morally, they believed that the bombing of North Vietnam was wrong. Innocent Vietnamese men, women, and children were dying because of Johnson's action, protesters believed. In general, doves believed that it was morally wrong to send U.S. troops to any conflict that did not directly threaten the United States.

The Civil Rights Movement

The American Civil War (1861–65) may have freed blacks from slavery, but white people kept blacks imprisoned in a world of discrimination and bigotry for nearly a century after the war ended. Although the U.S. Constitution's Bill of Rights formally guaranteed civil rights to every American, blacks remained second-class citizens well into the 1950s. In the Deep South, for example, blacks had to sit in the backs of buses. They were refused service at many lunch counters and forced to drink at water fountains marked "colored." Blacks were also forced to attend separate, poorly equipped schools, and they were often denied the right to vote.

Although civil rights groups like the National Association for the Advancement of Colored People (NAACP) had been formed early in the century, the civil rights movement began in earnest in the 1950s when more and more black people and a growing number of white people challenged the morality of denying blacks basic civil rights.

A major step toward civil rights for blacks was taken in 1954 when the U.S. Supreme Court outlawed segregation in schools. But the South responded slowly to the order. At some schools, federal troops were required to keep order when black students enrolled in them.

In 1957, black minister Martin Luther King led a successful boycott against bus lines of Montgomery, Alabama, which allowed blacks to sit only in the backs of buses. The boycott's success catapulted King to the forefront of the civil rights movement. King advocated nonviolent methods to gain civil rights.

In response to all the protests, Congress passed the Civil Rights Act in 1964. This act forbade discrimination in the use of most public facilities. A year later, a new law helped guarantee blacks their right to vote.

But making laws was one thing and changing society's attitudes was another. In 1965, riots broke out in the Watts section of Los Angeles, where blacks lived. The riots broke out because the new laws had not been translated into real programs to stem high unemployment and poor living conditions in the ghetto. Blacks still had no sense of hope about their futures.

In 1966, a split developed among black leaders of the civil rights movement. While Martin Luther King continued to advocate working for civil rights using nonviolent methods, other leaders like Stokely Carmichael became disenchanted with the slowness of nonviolent methods. Carmichael and others were further enraged by continued violence against blacks. On June 12, 1963, NAACP secretary Medgar Evers was murdered in his home in Jackson, Mississippi. On September 15 of the same year, four young black girls were killed in a church bombing in Birmingham, Alabama. Carmichael advocated violence to achieve civil rights goals. His point seemed to be underscored on April 4, 1968, when Martin Luther King himself was assassinated by a white man. King's death touched off more riots throughout the country.

Martin Luther King Jr. (center, front) locks arms with fellow marchers at a 1963 civil rights rally in Washington, D.C.

Strategically, protesters claimed involvement in Vietnam was unnecessary. The war was a civil war between the South Vietnamese government and the Communist-supported Vietcong, protesters claimed, and the United States should not get involved. Vietnam and its neighboring countries, poor Third World nations, were not important to the United States, doves argued. Even if Vietnam did fall to communism, doves believed, it would not be harmful to the security of the United States.

The earliest doves of the war made their antiwar views known with small, peaceful protests. For example, in April 1965, shortly after Johnson sent troops to Vietnam, twenty-five hundred members of the clergy used what was then a traditional and accepted form of protest. They took out a full-page advertisement in the *New York Times* to protest Johnson's action. The advertisement demanded that the president "In the name of God STOP IT."

About the same time, students at Columbia University in New York City sent a message to North Vietnamese leader Ho Chi Minh saying, "We are Americans who are deeply opposed to the U.S. bombing raids against the people of [North Vietnam]. We are doing all that we can to stop these barbarous attacks."

It was not the fashion in the spring of 1965 to speak out against the government. Early protesters were called peaceniks and Vietniks by the media.

Frank Emspak, one of two men who founded the National Coordinating Committee to End the War in Vietnam, speaks to reporters in 1965.

Hawks and Doves

The media used two very different kinds of birds, the warlike hawk and the peaceful dove, to characterize people's views on Vietnam. Hawks took a prowar position on America's role in Vietnam, while doves were opposed to getting further involved.

Together hawks and doves played an important role in the formation of Vietnam policies. In making decisions about Vietnam, President Johnson and later President Richard M. Nixon tried to please both hawks and doves. Since hawks and doves held opposite viewpoints about the war, each president's course of action was somewhere in the middle in order to avoid angering either side too much. In trying to please both sides, neither president pursued a policy strong enough to bring about an early end to the war.

To please both hawks and doves, President Johnson slowly escalated the Vietnam War. By escalating the war, the president was trying to show hawks that America was committed to South Vietnam. By escalating it a little bit at a time, he was trying to keep doves from getting too angry. In the end the slow escalation of the war failed to achieve America's goals.

The Berrigan Brothers

Catholic priests Daniel and Philip Berrigan were among the most active and committed protesters of the Vietnam War. Their radical actions and the punishment they received for these actions illustrate how strong antiwar feelings were in America.

The Berrigans opposed the war from its beginning. Their early protests were peaceful, but as the war continued, their protests became more radical. On October 27, 1967, Philip and three others entered the draft board office in the Customs House in Baltimore, Maryland, and poured duck's blood on draft records. Philip was tried and convicted of defacing government property and interfering with the functioning of the selective service system. Philip wrote of his actions to a friend:

> To stop this war I would give my life tommorrow. I believe in revolution, and I hope to continue a non-violent contribution to it. In my view, we are not going to save this country and mankind without it…the massive suffering of this war and American imperialism around the world will only be confronted by the people who are willing to go with suffering as the first move to justice.

While waiting to be sentenced, Philip and his brother Daniel planned a second protest. On May 17, 1968, the Berrigan brothers and seven others entered the draft board office in Cantonsville, Maryland. As surprised clerks stood by, they emptied hundreds of 1-A draft records into wire wastebaskets. They carried the baskets to the parking lot and set them afire using homemade napalm.

The Cantonsville Nine, as they became known, were tried for conspiracy and destruction of government property. On the witness stand, Daniel Berrigan explained his actions: "I

The Rev. Philip F. Berrigan (center) and his brother Rev. Daniel Berrigan (right) are shown throwing matches on the already burning draft records in Baltimore.

burned some paper because I was trying to say that the burning of children was inhuman and unbearable…."

The Cantonsville Nine were convicted. Daniel was sentenced to three years in prison, Philip three and one-half years, which was to be served at the same time as the six years he received for his first draft board conviction.

On March 9, 1970, the day they were to begin their prison sentences, the Berrigan brothers went into hiding. Their freedom did not last long. Philip was captured on April 21, Daniel on August 11. The Berrigans served their prison sentences, and after their release, continued to work for social change.

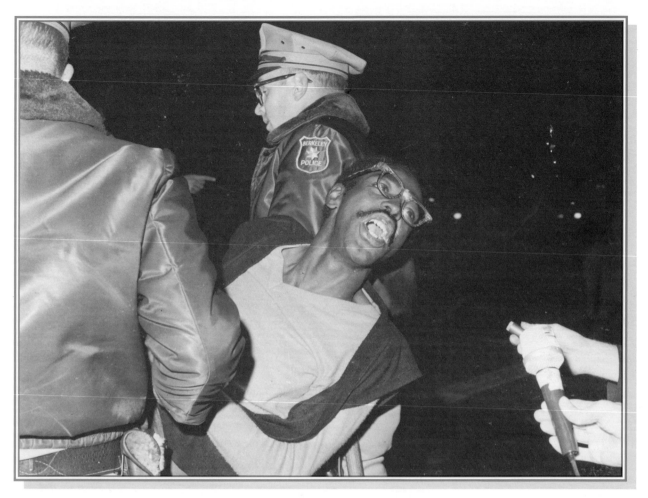

A protester is dragged by police to a waiting patrol car after a 1966 antiwar demonstration in Berkeley, California. Similar events occurred around the nation.

Protests Escalate

As Johnson's escalation of U.S. involvement in the war continued, protests against the war escalated as well. Many more people became involved, and the protests were not limited to small gestures like advertisements and messages.

By fall of 1965, an organization called The National Coordinating Committee to End the War in Vietnam had been created by two Wisconsin protesters, Frank Emspak and Ray Robinson. On October 15, this committee helped to organize simultaneous antiwar protests in forty cities around the United States. Ten thousand protesters marched in New York City, while twelve thousand marched in Berkeley, California. The emergence of a national organization to protest the war indicated that the protest movement was much stronger and more organized than it had been the previous spring.

But hawks were just as united in supporting America's war effort. In the New York march, hawks dashed antiwar protesters with red paint and pelted them with eggs. Hawks threw red paint to symbolize communism. They believed protesters were supporting communism by criticizing U.S. policy.

The growing split in America's feelings about the war in the fall of 1965 was evident between students at the University of Michigan in Ann Arbor. About 250 protesters from the university held a sit-in demonstration at the Ann Arbor selective service headquarters, where men enlisted or were drafted into the service. (A sit-in was a nonviolent form of protest where demonstrators sat down on the floor until their demands were met or they were arrested and carried away.) Back on campus, however, 2,057 students and teachers sent President Johnson a thirty-two-foot-long telegram supporting his efforts to "bring about a viable peace in Vietnam."

The Military Draft

The military draft was an immediate target of war protesters. The draft was the system by which soldiers were selected for required military service. The draft was administered by the selective service system. Under its rules, men eighteen years of age were required to register at their local selective service office. They received a draft card that listed their classification, or eligibility, for service. When the government needed additional soldiers, it called up, or drafted, men who were classified as 1-A. Classification 1-A meant that a male was eligible for induction.

The military draft was criticized by antiwar protesters for several reasons. Draft protesters resented the fact that it directed very young men to serve in Vietnam. The average age of the World War II soldier had been twenty-six years. But with the draft, the average age of the Vietnam War soldier was only nineteen years. Many Americans felt that nineteen was too young to be exposed to the horrors of war.

Draft protesters also claimed that the draft discriminated against poor blacks, Hispanics, and other minorities. Because college students could apply to be released from the draft, and because the majority of college students were white, protesters believed minorities were unfairly drafted in greater numbers. Protesters also opposed the draft because they opposed the war.

Selective service offices were located in cities and towns all over the country. Protesters had a physical target upon which to demonstrate their objections to the war. Some draft protesters broke into selective service offices and poured blood on the draft records to symbolize the blood of Americans being spilled in Vietnam. In other cases, draft registration records were burned

Rock-and-Roll

Rock-and-roll was born in the 1950s. It was energetic, sexy, and loud, and it had a beat. Many parents hated it and felt threatened by it. Many of their children, therefore, loved it. Rock-and-roll became the new generation's medium for self-expression and communication.

During the sixties, rock and roll came of age and developed a social conscience. Through music, young people believed they could change the world. Though the music itself was still the most important message, rock-and-roll lyrics often attacked major social issues of the day, including the Vietnam War. Song lyrics reflected America's changing and conflicting attitudes about the war.

In August 1969, the Woodstock Music and Art Fair in Woodstock, New York, brought nearly a half million young people together for three days of fun and music. Country Joe McDonald took the stage dressed in a green army jacket and a headband and led the crowd in a rousing version of his antiwar song "I-Feel-Like-I'm-Fixing-to-Die-Rag." The chorus accurately summed up most young people's attitude about fighting in the war:

Thousands of young people gathered in Woodstock, New York, in August 1969 for three days of fun and music. Much of the music reflected concerns about the Vietnam War.

> And it's one, two, three,
> What are we fightin' for?
> Don't ask me I don't give a damn,
> My next stop is Vietnam,
> And it's five, six, seven,
> Open up the pearly gates,
> Well, ain't no time to wonder why,
> Whoopie we're all gonna die.

in the hope that the U.S. government could not draft the men whose records were destroyed.

Other protesters burned their draft cards to oppose the war. The U.S. government made burning draft cards a federal crime in August of 1965, but the new law did not stop the practice. In mid-October, twenty-two-year-old David Miller announced at a protest rally in New York City, "I believe the napalming of villages in Vietnam is an immoral act. I hope this will be a significant political act, so here goes." He then set fire to his draft card. Three days later he was arrested. Miller became the first person convicted of burning his draft card. He was sentenced to three years in jail.

But not everyone protested the draft. Many Americans held to the time-honored belief that it was a man's duty to serve his country in time of need. Parents were often at odds with their

Four young men burn their draft cards to protest American involvement in Vietnam.

children over the draft. In particular, fathers who had served in World War II and Korea often could not understand why their sons objected to joining the service and defending their country.

Facing the Draft

All young men were required to sign up for the draft at the age of eighteen. If they were drafted, they faced the possibility of serving in Vietnam. Most men followed tradition and joined the military when drafted.

But other men felt that their moral beliefs prevented them from serving in the military. Michael Wanchena explains why he personally felt he could not fight in the Vietnam War: "From my earliest memories, I had been taught to respect all life. I had been taught that God lives in each one of us, that we were temples of His spirit. If I harmed my brothers, or sisters, or friends, I was harming God."

Whatever their reasons were, there were numerous ways that men could avoid the draft. Some acquired student deferments and went to college to avoid being drafted.

Other men became draft dodgers and fled the country, often hiding in Canada or Sweden. Once a draft dodger left the United States, he was regarded as a criminal by the U.S. government and faced imprisonment if he ever returned to the United States, even to visit family.

A small number of men asked the selective service to classify them as conscientious objectors. Conscientious objectors are people whose beliefs, usually religious, prevent them from fighting in their country's armed forces. Some conscientious objectors agreed to serve in the military in noncombat functions. They were usually resented by other soldiers and given the worst kinds of duties as a punishment for their beliefs. Other conscientious objectors refused military service of any kind and went to prison rather than violate their beliefs.

No matter what a man decided about the draft, his decision drew criticism from someone. Men who accepted induction into the military and served their country in Vietnam were often blamed for the war when they returned home. They were sometimes spat upon by war protesters and branded as murderers and baby killers.

Draft protesters, draft dodgers, and conscientious objectors were often labeled by those who supported the war as cowards or traitors. Recalls conscientious objector Michael Wanchena, "I suffered for my beliefs. I was rejected by men and women...and by most of my family.... Some said, and many thought, that I was a coward."

The media brought images of the war home in vivid and disturbing detail as can be seen in this July 1965 Life *magazine photograph of frightened civilians caught in a battle between Vietcong and South Vietnamese forces.*

The War, the Media, and the Credibility Gap

During the Vietnam War, President Johnson lost his credibility with the American people by not being honest with them. First, Johnson campaigned for reelection as a peace candidate. After reelection he increased U.S. involvement in Vietnam. But he kept details of the number of troops in Vietnam a secret because he feared his actions would be unpopular with the American people. His instincts were correct. When the public learned about the escalation, many Americans who had voted for Johnson felt betrayed by his dishonesty. The fact that he had waited nearly a month before he made his actions public angered many even further and made them suspicious of him.

Johnson routinely kept what was really going on in Vietnam a secret. Each month he sent more troops to Vietnam to keep the South Vietnamese government from losing the war. Yet at the same time, Johnson and his administration gave Americans the impression that the war effort was going well.

While the Johnson administration was painting a positive picture of the Vietnam War, the media were reporting a much different version. Newspaper and magazine articles chronicled the deaths of Americans, the frustrations of American soldiers, and the death and devastation caused by American bombs and napalm.

Television covered the war in a way that war had never been covered before. Reporters filmed their stories and had them flown home for broadcast. Live-action footage of events that were only hours old were beamed right into the living rooms of Americans. Never before had Americans been brought so close to the field of battle, and they were shocked and sickened by what they saw. Seeing the bloodied, dead bodies of American soldiers and horrifying scenes of bombed-out villages right in their living rooms turned even more Americans against the war.

Many Americans, even ones who supported Johnson, had trouble reconciling what they saw on television with Johnson's version of the war. By the end of 1965, the media had coined the

The sight of soldiers dragging a wounded comrade to safety and the rising toll of dead and wounded helped turn more and more Americans against the war.

Scenes, like this one, of a young girl holding a baby, her home ruined, shocked and sickened Americans.

term "credibility gap" to describe the difference between what Johnson had been telling Americans about the war and what reporters were reporting.

However, instead of narrowing the credibility gap, Johnson managed only to widen it. By 1967, it was clear that the war was at a stalemate. Though he knew better, Johnson continued to reassure Americans that the war was going well in an effort to keep support for his policies. In the fall of 1967, for example, Johnson had General Westmoreland issue a statement that the war was nearly over and that Americans would soon be coming home.

Widening Protests

The widening of the credibility gap encouraged support for the protest movement. In the fall of 1967, the protest movement was front-page news, along with the war itself. In October more than forty thousand protesters gathered in Washington, D.C., and picketed the Pentagon, the headquarters of the U.S. military. The event, along with coverage of similar protests in many other

American cities, was the cover story of *Time* magazine's October 27, 1967, issue. The march on the Pentagon, *Time* acknowledged, drew protesters from all walks of life:

> Within the tide of dissenters swarmed all the elements of American dissent in 1967: hard-eyed revolutionaries and sky-larking hippies; ersatz motorcycle gangs and all-too-real college professors; housewives, ministers and authors; Black Nationalists in African garb...[and] non-violent pacifists.

People's reasons for protesting the war had expanded beyond just moral and strategic grounds. Protesters believed the war was ruining the country. Young American soldiers were dying at alarming rates. Every week body bags carrying dead soldiers were shipped back to the United States.

People turned against Johnson's policies. They could see on their television sets that America was not winning in Vietnam. Yet Johnson spoke of winning. America's motives had become so confusing that many Americans no longer understood why men were being sent to Vietnam to die.

Americans also turned against Johnson because the war was hurting the U.S. economy. America had enjoyed prosperous times since 1961. But the war was so expensive that the country was having trouble paying for it. Government programs to help the poor and the needy were cut back to pay for the war. Inflation drove prices up for everyone.

The Turning Point

The war protests left Johnson feeling as though he were fighting two wars, one in Vietnam and one in his own country. The mood of the country had changed over the past three years. In March of 1968, a public opinion poll showed that 49 percent, almost half, of the American public viewed the war as "a mistake."

After seeing the poll, Johnson knew he had to end the war in Vietnam quickly to satisfy the American people. At the same time, he wanted to convince North Vietnam that America was still determined to achieve its goals in Vietnam.

On March 31, 1968, as the Tet Offensive was still subsiding, President Johnson spoke to America in a nationally televised address. He announced a dramatic new policy that he hoped would please those who were opposed to the war and still give him a chance to achieve his own goal.

The United States, Johnson told his television audience, would negotiate rather than fight with North Vietnam to end the war and achieve peace in Vietnam:

> We ask that talks begin promptly, that they be serious talks on the substance of peace. We are prepared to move immediately toward peace through negotiations.... I am taking

the first step to deescalate the conflict. We are reducing—substantially reducing—the present level of hostilities. And we are doing so unilaterally, and at once.

At the end of the broadcast, the president made an even more startling announcement. "I shall not seek, and I will not accept, the nomination of my party for another term as your president." The past four years had been stressful for him and for America. A half million soldiers were serving in Vietnam, with no real end of the war in sight. The nation's economy was suffering. In many American cities, blacks were rioting for their civil rights. It was election year again. Johnson knew he had destroyed his credibility with the country and other leading Democrats were challenging him for the party's nomination for president. The president had had enough.

Johnson had finally listened to the American voices rising up in protest against the war, and he had recognized the failure of his military strategy in Vietnam. He had set the nation on a new course to achieve peace in both America and Vietnam. He was willing to step aside and let a new president lead the United States out of the terrible nightmare of the Vietnam War.

CHAPTER FOUR

The United States Leaves Vietnam

President Johnson's offer to negotiate with North Vietnam to achieve peace was the first step toward the end of U.S. involvement in Vietnam. But the road that led to the end of the Vietnam War for the United States would prove to be very long and arduous.

The Paris Peace Talks

The North Vietnamese accepted Johnson's negotiation offer on April 3, 1968. A feeling of optimism spread through America. After three long years of fighting, it looked like a break in what had become known as Johnson's War had finally occurred. A month later, North Vietnam and the United States agreed upon Paris, France, as the city in which the negotiations would be held.

Almost an entire year would pass, however, before negotiations would begin. North Vietnam stalled the talks, in part to gain time to rebuild its armies and continue the war. The North Vietnamese also knew it was an election year in the United States. The negotiators hoped they might get a better deal from a new president.

The negotiations finally got under way on January 25, 1969. Weeks, then months, went by, and with them, America's hopes for an early peace agreement. In fact, for the next three and one-half years, nothing would be resolved at the Paris Peace Talks, as each side clung to its goals and refused to make any concessions.

Henry Kissinger (center), special adviser to President Richard Nixon, speaks to reporters in November 1972 during one of many negotiating sessions with North Vietnamese representatives in Paris.

Nixon's Peace Strategies

Richard Nixon was sworn in as president of the United States on January 20, 1969, just before the peace talks began. He had defeated Hubert H. Humphrey in the closest presidential election in American history. During the campaign, Nixon had told Americans he had a peace plan that he would unveil after he became president.

Nixon wanted to achieve what he called an honorable peace in Vietnam. He was determined not to abandon Vietnam, as many Americans wanted him to do. To the president, it was also important that other countries continue to believe that the United States would keep its promises. Just withdrawing from Vietnam, Nixon believed, would destroy U.S. credibility with other countries and damage its world standing.

Nixon's program to achieve peace in Vietnam took shape slowly over a period of months. It had three main parts. First, Nixon wanted to turn the fighting of the war back over to the South Vietnamese people, a process he called Vietnamization. This policy continued Johnson's promise that he would get the United States out of Vietnam. Second, Nixon planned to expand the war into other countries in an effort to bring it to a quicker end. Finally, Nixon attempted to improve relationships with China and the Soviet Union to help bring peace.

President Nixon and Vietnam

Although it took him nearly four years, President Nixon succeeded in ending U.S. involvement in Vietnam early in 1973. But in the eyes of many, Nixon's abuse of his powers in Vietnam and the Watergate scandal overshadow this accomplishment. Today Nixon is remembered less for ending the war than for being the only American president forced to resign from office. Congress and many Americans felt that Nixon abused his presidential power in Vietnam. This perception not only contributed to his downfall but also led to legislation that weakened the presidency.

Throughout his four-year effort to end U.S. involvement in Vietnam, Nixon sought to sidestep congressional authority. For example, after Nixon announced details of the Cambodian invasion in 1970, Congress revoked the Gulf of Tonkin Resolution that had given President Johnson authority to defend U.S. personnel in Vietnam.

But Nixon continued to use U.S. troops and air power as he felt necessary to bring the war to an end. At the very minimum, Nixon violated Congress's wishes if not any actual laws.

In 1973, it was discovered that Nixon had lied to both Congress and the public about Vietnam. Soon after taking office in 1969 and again early in 1970, Nixon had ordered secret bombings in Cambodia. Pentagon records were falsified to cover up the bombings.

President Nixon finally ended U.S. involvement in Vietnam in 1973.

This discovery further outraged Congress. To reclaim some of its own power and to limit the power of the president to wage war, Congress passed the War Powers Act on November 7, 1973. The act prohibited Nixon and all future presidents from committing U.S. troops overseas for more than sixty days without congressional authority.

Nixon had always been a decisive president who was willing to make unpopular decisions and stand by them. By sidestepping Congress, Nixon was trying to strengthen his own power. Ironically, his efforts left succeeding presidents with even less power.

Vietnamization

Nixon began to Vietnamize the war soon after taking office. The United States attempted to improve the South Vietnamese army so that it could once again assume the fighting. As the Vietnamization process proceeded, American troops would be withdrawn from the fighting and brought home.

Nixon hoped that Vietnamization would reduce the number of American casualties in Vietnam. With fewer Americans dying in Vietnam and troops coming home, there would be less pressure on him from within America to withdraw immediately. Nixon hoped this would give him time to pursue the peace with honor settlement he wanted.

In June of 1969, Nixon ordered 25,000 American troops to withdraw from Vietnam. More troops came home in September and December, bringing the total number of troops withdrawn to 115,000 in 1969. More troops were withdrawn early in 1970.

These young women, members of the People's Self-Defense Force of Kien Dien, patrol their village to discourage Vietcong infiltration.

Young men from South Vietnam's forty-four provinces trained for thirteen weeks and then returned to their homes to help villagers defend themselves against the Vietcong.

Expanding the War

The second part of Nixon's strategy was to destroy Communist sanctuaries in neighboring countries that supplied the North Vietnamese war effort in South Vietnam. Nixon hoped reversing Johnson's decision to limit the war would help him succeed where Johnson had failed. Johnson's limited war had prevented U.S. troops from entering Cambodia and Laos to destroy Communist troops and supplies. This had given the Communists an advantage that Nixon was determined to destroy.

Immediately after assuming office, Nixon authorized secret bombing raids inside Cambodia to destroy Communist sanctuaries. He kept the raids secret because he did not think the American public would understand how his policies would help end the war sooner.

Nixon's secret bombings did not destroy all the Communist troops and supplies in Cambodia, however. In the spring of 1970, Nixon took even stronger action. He authorized a ground invasion of Cambodia. South Vietnamese troops aided by American troops and air support crossed the border into Cambodia on

A soldier practices firing a grenade launcher at a training camp in Vietnam.

South Vietnamese troops, backed by the Americans, attacked North Vietnamese strongholds in Cambodia in 1970. Here, South Vietnamese soldiers rush to a helicopter during one such assault.

April 30 to completely destroy North Vietnamese supplies and troops. The invasion took Communist forces by surprise. They abandoned their South Vietnamese military headquarters and tons of supplies.

Nixon made the invasion of Cambodia public on April 30. The news outraged many Americans. They felt that Nixon's action was immoral and further escalated a war that he had promised to end.

The Cambodian invasion sparked the worst outbreak of antiwar protests that America had ever seen. College students in particular were enraged by Nixon's policy. Antiwar demonstrations were organized on most college campuses across the country. The target of many demonstrations was the campus office of the Reserve Officer Training Corps (ROTC). The ROTC was a college training program for future army reserve officers. For the angry students, the ROTC office symbolized the U.S. army, which they held responsible for the war. During antiwar demonstrations, ROTC buildings were burned on thirty college campuses.

The war demonstrations became too large and violent for local police to control. To restore order, the U.S. National Guard was called out to twenty-one universities across the country. The presence of National Guard troops on campus further

The Kent State Tragedy

President Nixon's expansion of the war into Cambodia on April 30, 1970, caused a national outburst of violent protests. One such protest on May 4 resulted in a confrontation between national guardsmen and students at Kent State University in Ohio.

The campus had been the scene of a weekend of protests. The ROTC headquarters had been burned down on Saturday evening, May 2. The city's mayor, LeRoy Satrom, had asked Ohio governor James Rhodes to send National Guard troops to restore order. The guard arrived late that night and took up positions on campus. On Sunday, May 3, the guardsmen broke up a student rally with bayonets.

On Monday, May 4, the students reassembled at noon on the campus commons to hold a rally. The students were told that the assembly was unlawful and were ordered to disperse. The students were incensed. They seemed to switch their attention from the war to the fact that the National Guard was on their campus. The students threw rocks at the guardsmen, and the guardsmen fired tear gas into the crowds. The guardsmen then went through the commons and returned to their original position at 12:24 P.M. Suddenly, according to witnesses, the guardsmen turned and started firing into the crowd. Thirteen seconds later, the shooting stopped. Four students lay dead or dying, and nine more were wounded.

The deaths of the four students rocked America and sparked even more protests. Students went on strike on hundreds of campuses across the nation. Many campuses were closed for the rest of the school year. More than seventy-five thousand protesters marched on Washington, D.C., on May 9.

To an ever-increasing number of Americans, the deaths at Kent State symbolized what was wrong with U.S. involvement in Vietnam. These deaths were unnecessary and senseless. The tragedy somehow proved that everything protesters had been saying about their government was right.

Masked National Guardsmen fire a barrage of tear gas into a crowd of antiwar demonstrators at Kent State University in Ohio.

enraged the students. At a confrontation between guardsmen and students at Kent State University in Ohio, four students were killed, and nine more were wounded. The deaths in America continued. Ten days later, two students were killed by police in racial riots at Jackson State University in Mississippi.

Congress Reacts

Congress also reacted negatively to Nixon's invasion of Cambodia. On June 24, the Senate voted to repeal the 1964 Gulf of Tonkin Resolution, which had given President Johnson authority to send troops to Vietnam. Six days later, the Senate passed an amendment barring further U.S. military action in Cambodia.

In 1971, Nixon continued his expansion strategy despite protests by Congress and the American public. On February 8, the South Vietnamese army crossed into Laos to destroy Communist sanctuaries there. The Lam Son 719 Campaign, as the Laos operation was called, met with disaster. This time the Communists knew in advance of the planned invasion and devastated South Vietnamese troops. The South Vietnamese army would

South Vietnamese paratroopers march through tall grass after crossing into Laos to destroy Communist strongholds.

The My Lai Killings

On the morning of March 16, 1968, Lt. William Calley Jr. led his platoon into the hamlet of My Lai in search of enemy Vietcong. The Vietcong had been very active in the area, killing or wounding many American troops, then quickly disappearing. Instead of the enemy, Calley and his men found old men, women, and children in the village. Calley had been taught to suspect any Vietnamese as a potential enemy. His orders were to destroy the enemy. He gave the order to attack. Grenades were thrown into huts. Some villagers were shot down in their homes or where they stood. Others were herded to a nearby drainage ditch and shot down with automatic weapons. Before the morning ended, Calley and his men had killed between three hundred and five hundred villagers.

It was nearly two years before a shocked American public learned of the killings at My Lai. Twenty-five officers and enlisted men were eventually charged with the killings. In all but one case, the charges were either dismissed or the soldiers were acquitted.

For his part in the My Lai killings, Lieutenant Calley was court-martialed and tried during 1970 and 1971. Calley maintained that he was simply following orders. His defense raised the question of whether following orders could excuse soldiers from having to make moral decisions. It also raised the question of whether superior officers could be held responsible for the acts of their men.

The trial left America divided about My Lai and the issues it raised. Calley was viewed as both a murderer who deserved punishment for his horrible crimes and as a scapegoat who was being blamed and punished for all of America's involvement in the war.

The military court found Calley guilty of murdering at least twenty-two villagers. He was sentenced to life in prison, but after three days in the stockade, he was released by President Nixon and put under house arrest. Three years later, he was paroled.

The young boy pictured at the center of this photograph claimed he survived the My Lai massacre by hiding under dead bodies.

have been completely destroyed if U.S. air support had not been sent in to bomb the Communists while the South Vietnamese army retreated.

The complete failure of the Lam Son 719 Campaign made U.S. political and military leaders reevaluate Nixon's expansion strategy. Because the South Vietnamese army had been so badly beaten by the Communists, America's leaders also questioned whether the South Vietnamese could ever win without U.S. help.

Yet, even while critics debated whether expansion and Vietnamization worked, Nixon kept bringing American troops home as he had promised. By spring of 1971, only 284,000 troops remained in Vietnam, slightly more than half the number of troops stationed there when he took office.

Detente

The third part of Nixon's strategy to achieve peace with honor in Vietnam was to encourage detente, or a lessening of tensions, with the Soviet Union and China. In 1969, the United States opened talks with the Soviet Union on arms limitation. An agreement limiting arms for both countries was reached in May 1972. Nixon honored this agreement by accepting an invitation to visit Moscow.

In 1971, Nixon relaxed the United States' trade embargo against China. This was a significant step because the United States had had no diplomatic or trade relationship with China since the Communists had taken control of the country in 1949. In February 1972, Nixon traveled to China to meet with Chinese leaders. These talks opened new possibilities for trade and opened channels of communication that had been closed since 1949.

Nixon hoped that detente would accomplish two things. First, it would allow him to expand the war into Cambodia and Laos without drawing in the Soviet Union or China. Johnson had feared that either country would get involved if he expanded the war beyond South Vietnam. Through detente, Nixon determined that as long as he did not try to invade North Vietnam and overthrow its government, China and the Soviet Union would stay out of the war.

Second, Nixon hoped that detente would encourage the Soviet Union and China to pressure North Vietnam to end the war. He wanted both countries to view the Vietnam War as a stumbling block to more important issues. In his meetings with both countries, Nixon linked trade and other agreements to the resolution of the Vietnam War. If the Soviet Union and China would act to resolve the Vietnam War, Nixon hinted, these agreements could be worked out.

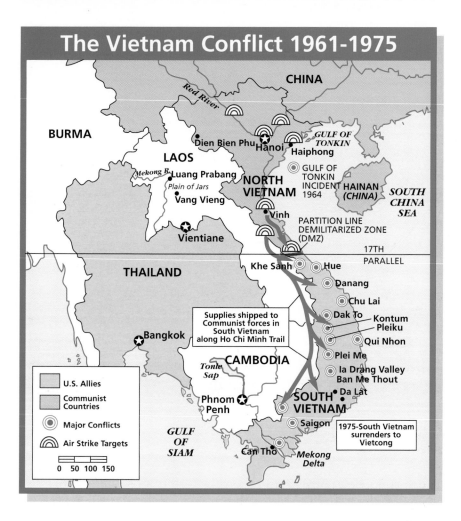

The Vietnam Conflict 1961-1975

Detente as a strategy took a long time to implement. Most of Nixon's critics concede that detente improved the United States' relationship with each country. But critics remain divided over whether Nixon's detente strategy actually helped him end the Vietnam War earlier.

The Spring Offensive

As Nixon struggled to make his three-pronged strategy to end the Vietnam War work, the war suddenly took a different twist. North Vietnamese General Giap had recognized the failure of Vietnamization and he knew that Nixon hoped for a peace settlement before he faced reelection in the fall of 1972. A successful North Vietnamese offensive, Giap hoped, would destroy the South Vietnamese army for good. It also might force the United States into a quick peace settlement with terms that favored North Vietnam. Finally, if successful, the offensive would leave North Vietnam in control of large areas of South Vietnam.

On March 30, 1972, Giap launched a massive offensive

Battle-weary South Vietnamese soldiers cheer as reinforcements arrive at the besieged provincial capital of An Loc.

against South Vietnam. North Vietnamese troops began a massive barrage of artillery fire along the South Vietnamese border. Hours later forty thousand North Vietnamese troops and two hundred tanks drove across the border into South Vietnam. The North Vietnamese Communists soon took control of many towns and villages, forcing the South Vietnamese army to retreat.

Some of the hardest fighting occurred at An Loc, a provincial capital only sixty miles from the national capital of Saigon. The Communists first seized control of An Loc on April 8. For the next three weeks, the battle for An Loc continued, often with hand-to-hand fighting. On May 3, a South Vietnamese relief force fought its way through the town and drove the North Vietnamese out.

Between May and September, the South Vietnamese army, aided by the U.S. Air Force, slowly retook the towns lost to the North Vietnamese in the early days of the spring offensive. General Giap was denied a victory over the South Vietnamese. But the South Vietnamese victory was a hollow one. Though the South Vietnamese had fought hard and bravely, it was the U.S. Air Force that actually broke the offensive. These battles once again reinforced the fact that the South Vietnamese government could not survive without massive U.S. military aid.

North Vietnamese negotiator Le Duc Tho greets reporters in 1972 in Paris, where he and Henry Kissinger conducted a series of peace talks.

Serious Negotiations

The peace talks begun in 1969 had continued without progress. Early in 1970, Nixon had determined that the delicate negotiations necessary to end the war could not be accomplished in the public peace talks. He sent his national security adviser Henry Kissinger on a secret mission to meet with North Vietnamese negotiator Le Duc Tho in an effort to negotiate a peace. Kissinger and Tho had met for two years without finding a way to break the deadlock in the talks.

But in mid-1972, as the Spring Offensive continued, peace negotiations suddenly became serious. Both sides were ready to make compromises. In the United States, Nixon recognized that diplomacy now offered the best hope for peace. The Spring Offensive had pointed out that South Vietnam could not win the war without continued U.S. involvement. Nixon's inability to end the war had eroded his support at home. As the 1972 election drew nearer, Nixon knew he would have to show some type of progress on the road to peace if he were to win reelection.

The Communists were also willing to negotiate. They had suffered severe losses in the Spring Offensive. The peace talks would allow them to take a break in the war and rebuild their forces. If North Vietnam could negotiate a settlement to get American troops out of South Vietnam, they believed they could eventually defeat South Vietnam and unify the North and South.

Peace at Hand

Kissinger and Tho began serious negotiations in July. By October 8, they had worked out an agreement. A cease-fire would be announced for all Southeast Asia. The United States would withdraw its troops within sixty days. South Vietnamese leader Thieu would be allowed to remain in power. U.S. prisoners of war would be returned. The various Vietnamese parties would be left to themselves to decide about elections and the future of South Vietnam. The United States made one major concession. Some North Vietnamese troops would be allowed to stay in the South.

Even though Kissinger and Tho's proposal had taken months to negotiate and both sides had made concessions, South Vietnamese President Thieu rejected the proposal. Thieu opposed any kind of settlement because he knew he needed American support to stay in power, and the agreement was paving the way for the United States to leave Vietnam.

In October 1972, Kissinger and Tho worked out an agreement to end the war, but it was rejected by the South Vietnamese government.

President Nixon began to have second thoughts about the proposal. He feared that the agreement might not be tough enough to please the hawks who had long supported America's involvement in Vietnam. Using Thieu's protests about the proposal as an excuse, Nixon ordered Kissinger to continue the secret negotiations.

Kissinger's new negotiations made Tho fear that the United States was backing out of the proposal. To try to hold the United States to the agreement, Tho made the secret negotiations public. Tho's bold move forced Kissinger to declare prematurely that "peace was at hand," on October 26, in order to prevent the United States from being blamed for the snag in the peace talks.

But peace was not yet at hand. When the talks resumed after the 1972 election, which Nixon won in a landslide, each side concluded that the other was trying to back out of the agreement and the talks broke down on December 13.

Nixon and Kissinger's peace efforts were now threatened by both North and South Vietnam. To reassure his ally Thieu that America would stand behind him, Nixon offered two billion dollars' worth of military arms and supplies. He promised to come to South Vietnam's aid if North Vietnam violated the agreement. When Thieu still refused, Nixon warned him that the

The January 1973 peace treaty set up a prisoner exchange that led to the return of captured soldiers. Here, Lt. Col. James L. Hughes of Iowa, one of many prisoners of war, is escorted to a news conference in Hanoi in 1967.

The Vought A-7 Corsair II (left) was one of many jets used in bombing runs over Vietnam as were B-66 Destroyers and Air Force F-105 Thunderchiefs (right).

United States might sign a peace treaty whether he did or not. Thieu gave in, knowing he had no alternative.

Nixon next warned North Vietnam that it would suffer grave consequences if what he referred to as "serious negotiations" did not resume. On December 18, President Nixon made good on his threat. He ordered a massive bombing campaign against North Vietnam, including the capital city of Hanoi and the port city of Haiphong. For the next twelve days, except for one day off at Christmas, U.S. bombers hammered North Vietnam.

The American public was furious with Nixon. Once again, Nixon seemed to be escalating the war, and at a time when the country seemed on the verge of signing a peace treaty. Americans found it especially horrifying that Nixon would order bombing during the Christmas holiday. Congress also joined the protest. A poll taken a few days after the bombings began showed that nearly half of the Senate favored legislation to end the war.

The talks resumed again in early January of 1973. How effective the Christmas bombings were in convincing North Vietnam to resume the talks is still debated. The negotiations that followed changed some of the wording of the October proposal but not its basic content.

On January 27, a peace treaty very similar to the October proposal was signed. It called for American forces to withdraw from Vietnam sixty days after the signing. U.S. bases were to be dismantled, and the two sides would exchange prisoners of war.

U.S. bombers caused massive destruction to the North Vietnamese port city of Haiphong (left), and to a rail and highway bridge (right) that formed a major link between Hanoi and Haiphong.

The agreement also contained a complicated cease-fire between North Vietnam and South Vietnam that was to be overseen by two separate and neutral commissions.

The treaty ended the United States' longest war. The final twenty-seven thousand U.S. troops departed for home on March 29, 1973. Unable to defeat the Communists, the United States had negotiated itself out of the war, just as the French had done after the battle of Dien Bien Phu nineteen years earlier.

Members of the U.S. Ninth Infantry Division receive farewell gifts in a ceremony before their departure from Vietnam.

The Fall of South Vietnam

The Paris Peace Accords ended the war only for the United States. Both North and South Vietnam realized that the United States had negotiated the Paris Accords primarily to allow it to withdraw from Vietnam without admitting defeat. Each government soon gave up trying to maintain the cease-fire, and the fighting resumed. In the first year of "peace," renewed fighting killed eighty thousand Vietnamese people and soldiers.

The task the South Vietnamese faced was immense. They now had to defeat the Communists without help, something that they had been unable to do in nine years with the aid of up to 500,000 American troops. Although South Vietnam's forces were almost four times larger than the Communists' forces and were well equipped, they were poorly led. Their use of American arms and supplies was ineffective.

President Thieu remained unpopular with his people. Without American support, his government began to deteriorate. He was forced to use the army to maintain his power, which reduced its effectiveness in defending the country from the Communists.

When U.S. troops left Vietnam, South Vietnamese troops retreated from the advancing Communists.

South Vietnamese soldiers keep watch over two comrades, one dead and one wounded, as they await evacuation from the central highlands.

As his government deteriorated, Thieu continued to look to the United States for aid, convinced that his old ally would not abandon him.

But in America support for Vietnam had all but disappeared. Americans were tired of Vietnam, and few people seemed to care what was happening there.

The Vietnam War had caused a bitter dispute between Congress and the president over who ran foreign policy. During 1973, Congress passed three pieces of legislation that reduced the support the United States could give to South Vietnam, and took power away from Nixon. On June 29, Congress passed a bill imposing a total ban on U.S. bombing in all of Indochina after August 15. On August 6, Congress cut aid to South Vietnam to $700 million.

Congress felt that both Johnson and Nixon had abused their presidential powers in running the Vietnam War, and they wanted to establish congressional control over the president's power to wage war. The War Powers Act, passed by Congress on November 7, 1973, prevented the president from sending U.S. combat troops to any foreign country for more than sixty days without congressional approval.

But for Nixon, Vietnam had become an issue of minor importance during 1973. He had become embroiled in a huge political scandal known as Watergate and was struggling to stay in office. In June of 1972, five men had been caught burglarizing the national headquarters of the Democratic Party at the Watergate Hotel in Washington, D.C. The media soon linked the burglars to Nixon's campaign, but Nixon publicly denied any knowledge of the incident. Whether he knew about the burglary in advance is uncertain. But investigations carried on throughout 1973 by the media and Congress determined that soon after the break-in, Nixon had ordered his staff to cover up the event and stonewall efforts to learn the truth. On May 9, 1974, the Judiciary Committee of the House of Representatives began hearings to see if Nixon should be impeached, or removed from office and tried by the Senate for illegally using his presidential powers to obstruct the Watergate investigation. Rather than face impeachment, Nixon resigned on August 9, 1974, the only president in U.S. history to resign.

Nixon was replaced by Gerald R. Ford. President Ford attempted to keep Nixon's promise not to abandon South Vietnam, but his powers to act had been sharply limited by Congress.

The Communists knew that the United States would not send combat troops to Vietnam again. At the end of 1974, they set up a two-year, two-step program to achieve total victory in the South. During 1975, the Communists planned to launch continuous attacks against South Vietnam to weaken its resistance. Then in 1976, they would launch a large offensive and call for a general uprising by the South Vietnamese people against their government.

But the first part of the Communists' plan was far more successful than they had predicted. General Van Tien Dung, the head of the North Vietnamese army, left Hanoi on February 5 to take command of the offensive in South Vietnam. On March 9, the Communists attacked the South Vietnamese city of Ban Me Thuot in the central highlands. By March 10, they controlled the city.

The day after the Communists took control of Ban Me Thuot, Thieu met with his generals. Finally convinced that he would not receive any U.S. assistance, Thieu had decided to let the North Vietnamese take some of South Vietnam's northern provinces. Thieu hoped he could retreat and regroup his troops to defend the southern part of the country.

On March 15, the South Vietnamese army began to retreat from the city of Pleiku in the northern part of the central highlands toward the sea. The retreat became disorderly. Soldiers of all ranks deserted. A panic gripped the entire civilian population of South Vietnam. If the army was in retreat, then the war must be lost. Hundreds of thousands of fleeing refugees clogged the retreat route.

A South Vietnamese woman covers her eyes as she and others await a helicopter airlift out of Vietnam.

Graham Martin, U.S. ambassador to South Vietnam, ordered the evacuation of American diplomats and their families from Saigon in April 1975.

South Vietnam territories began to collapse like a row of falling dominoes. The Communists were scarcely able to occupy regions as fast as they were abandoned. In just two weeks, they took control of twelve provinces and eight million people. By April 26, the final campaign for the city of Saigon was ready. Total victory seemed only days away.

Although all U.S. combat troops had been withdrawn from Vietnam two years earlier, American diplomats and their families were still stationed at the American Embassy in Saigon. A signal was arranged to notify Americans when they would have to leave. When a local radio station began to play Bing Crosby's "White Christmas" over and over, everyone was to report immediately to the American embassy for evacuation. The U.S. government wanted the evacuation to remain secret to prevent panic and a possible storming of the embassy by South Vietnamese who wanted to leave Vietnam.

Thieu's plan to retreat and defend the southern part of the country failed. On April 29, Communists attacked the city of Saigon, and Graham Martin, U.S. ambassador to South Vietnam,

Americans and South Vietnamese jam the rooftops of Saigon buildings as they wait to be airlifted to safety by helicopters.

ordered the evacuation of Americans to begin. Crowds of terrified Americans and South Vietnamese people jammed the roof of the American embassy and other buildings in Saigon, waiting to be airlifted by helicopter to safety. The evacuation continued through the night as helicopters loaded with Americans and Vietnamese flew to nearby aircraft carriers. The final helicopter carrying Ambassador Martin, his family, and the American flag that had flown over the embassy lifted off the embassy roof at daybreak on the morning of April 30, 1975.

The Communists took control of Saigon on April 30. Their long struggle to reunite North and South Vietnam had finally ended with victory. Despite its thirty-year effort, the United States had failed to achieve its original goal of keeping communism out of South Vietnam.

CHAPTER FIVE

The Legacy of the Vietnam War

Marine Jim Mason left Vietnam on Christmas Day in 1967. He was happy to come home, put the war behind him, and get on with his life. Yet more than twenty years later, when he walked along his own street at night, Jim Mason often glanced between houses for Vietcong soldiers. In his own back yard, he sometimes caught himself listening for the snap of a twig, a sign of approaching danger. The Vietnam War had stayed with Jim Mason all of those years, and although he didn't want it to, it had become a part of his life.

Even though it ended years ago, the Vietnam War left a legacy that has become a part of America in the same unhappy way it became a part of Jim Mason's life. The American people are still defining and trying to understand the Vietnam War.

How Vietnam Changed America

For the first time in its history, the United States as a nation had lost a war. The South had lost the American Civil War, and the Korean War was ended through negotiation. But the entire country lost the Vietnam War.

Losing in Vietnam changed Americans' attitudes about themselves and their country's role in the world. Before Vietnam, most Americans believed that the United States should take an active role in world affairs. They especially believed that the United States should stem the spread of communism in other countries.

President Johnson, seen here greeting American troops in 1966, lost favor with the American public after he lied about actions in Vietnam.

After the Vietnam War American citizens questioned American involvement in other countries' affairs. Many Americans concluded that the United States should stop trying to impose its ideals on the rest of the world. They felt the United States should let other nations determine their own destinies and not send Americans to die for causes that do not threaten the United States.

Before the Vietnam War, Americans had a greater sense of trust in their leaders and in their government. They often supported the policies of their government officials even when they did not entirely agree with them. They did so because they trusted their leaders to know and do the right thing.

The Vietnam War shattered that trust. President Johnson had the support of much of America when he first sent troops to Vietnam early in 1965. But because he kept the details of his actions secret and lied to the very people who had elected him, the public started to question his honesty. When the news media exposed the credibility gap, Johnson did not admit to his deceptions. Instead, he continued to deceive the public in order to pursue a Vietnam policy that became more and more unpopular. The loss of his credibility was a major reason why he decided not to seek reelection in 1968.

President Nixon also caused Americans to distrust their leaders. Nixon's deceptive policies in Vietnam and his involvement in Watergate so destroyed Nixon's credibility that he was forced to resign.

As a result of Vietnam and the Watergate scandal, today America's leaders no longer enjoy the automatic trust of the American people. Politicians live in a bright spotlight, and their integrity is constantly questioned.

Much of this erosion of public trust can be traced to the news media. In the 1950s, the media respected public officials. The media protected their privacy and often shied away from scandal. During the Vietnam years the media exposed Johnson's and Nixon's dishonesty about Vietnam, which helped to change the way the media treated public officials. Today, the media view themselves as the public's watchdog. The media openly challenge the nation's public officials. Their private lives, once respected, are now routinely exposed. Scandal is fairly routine.

Vietnam Veterans

Nowhere is the legacy of the Vietnam War more keenly felt than in America's Vietnam veterans. In World Wars I and II, veterans had come home to parades and ceremonies. Vietnam soldiers came home to a country that blamed them for cooperating with the government in the war. Instead of being welcomed, people shunned, spat upon, and ridiculed Vietnam vets. Veterans felt ashamed, abandoned, and disowned. Many stopped telling people they were Vietnam veterans.

Those feelings were not the only problems that veterans encountered. Although most soldiers were able to resume their daily lives after they returned home, thousands of soldiers experienced a variety of emotional or physical illnesses caused by their service in Vietnam.

Like veterans of other wars, many suffered from a condition called posttraumatic stress disorder, or PTSD. PTSD is an emotional illness caused by a particular incident, such as combat, that creates great stress. Weeks, months, even years after they came home, veterans continued to think about or reexperience the things they had seen and done in Vietnam. Their whole lives and the lives of their families were affected by their continuing reaction to Vietnam.

Some veterans relived their experiences in nightmares or flashbacks. Others grew tense and jumpy at the sound of firecrackers, gunshots, or babies crying. Many lost interest in working and had trouble keeping jobs. In an effort to escape from the horror of their Vietnam experiences, others developed alcohol or drug habits. Hundreds of veterans became so mistrustful of other people that they withdrew from society altogether to live alone

The Vietnam Veterans Memorial

The Vietnam Veterans Memorial is one of the most popular tourist attractions in Washington, D.C., a city that is itself a monument to the nation. The memorial is the place where Americans come to mourn their loved ones lost in the war.

The memorial was conceived out of one man's pain. One night in 1979, Vietnam veteran Jan Scruggs experienced yet another nightmare about the war. The next morning, Scruggs determined that he would build a memorial that carried the name of every American who had died in the war. It took him nearly three years, but he accomplished his goal.

A contest was held to determine the design. The winning design was submitted by Maya Ying Lin, a 21-year-old Chinese-American architecture student. A spot in Constitution Gardens between the Washington Monument and the Lincoln Memorial was selected as the site. Construction began in March 1982.

The memorial consists of a long V-shaped wall of black Indian granite that rises out of the earth and then recedes back into it. Carved in the stone of this black wall are the names of the more than fifty-eight thousand Americans who died in Vietnam.

The memorial was dedicated on Veterans Day 1982. In 1984, a bronze sculpture of three weary soldiers in battle dress was added to satisfy veterans who wanted a more traditional memorial.

At all hours of the day, a steady stream of visitors solemnly files along the length of the long wall. Relatives and friends search for a special name. When they find it, they grow quiet. Tears stream down their faces as they reach out to touch the recessed letters. They often leave pictures of sons and daughters the soldiers never lived to meet. They leave flowers, poems, letters, and other mementos under the names of their lost loved ones. Many take sheets of white paper and with crayons make rubbings of the name to take home with them.

A soldier weeps for a lost comrade after finding his name on the black granite Vietnam Veterans Memorial in Washington, D.C.

A group of Vietnam veterans share an emotional reunion during a belated "Welcome Home" parade in Chicago in 1986.

in remote areas of Hawaii and other places. Some soldiers suffering from PTSD were even driven to suicide.

Raymond Earley returned from Vietnam in 1968. His feelings and postwar experiences echo those of many veterans who suffer from PTSD. In 1991, Earley still dreamed about picking up the charred bodies of American soldiers killed by the North Vietnamese. Earley spoke of his experiences:

> It's one of my nightmares. Twenty-three years after leaving Vietnam, I'm still learning how to relate to this. Sometimes I fantasize about what my life would be like if I hadn't gone to Vietnam. I don't like the way I feel, the way I relate [to things]. I had problems in the seventies with alcohol, authority and relationships. If I hadn't gone to Vietnam, maybe my life would have been different. People I went to school with are completely different from me. Maybe I would have a successful business and have stayed married to the girl I grew up with.

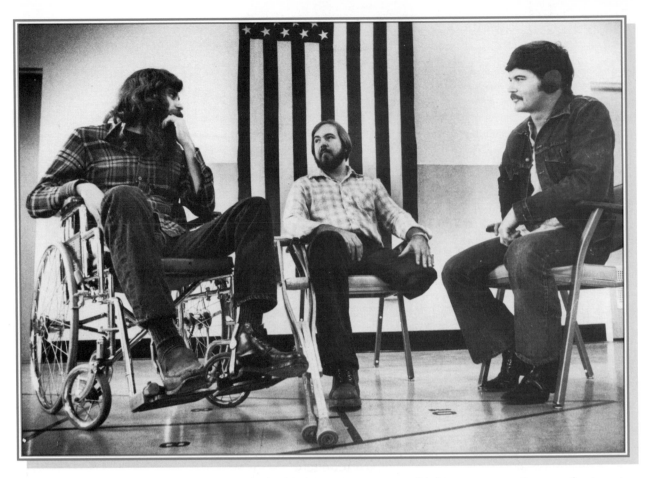

Many disabled Vietnam veterans felt bitterness over the way the American public and government treated them when they returned home from the war.

Emotional disorders are not the only health problems that plague Vietnam veterans. Many suffer from physical illnesses that they attribute to the war. During the Vietnam War, many veterans were exposed to the chemical Agent Orange. The United States sprayed eighteen million gallons of Agent Orange and other chemicals on the Vietnamese countryside to strip the leaves from trees and destroy crops. Medical studies have linked exposure to Agent Orange and similar chemicals to certain kinds of cancer. These chemicals have also been linked to birth defects.

No one knows for sure how many veterans were exposed to Agent Orange. After exposure doctors cannot tell which veterans will develop cancer. The disease can lie dormant in the human body for decades.

Although all veterans can receive free treatment at local veterans' hospitals, veterans claimed during the late 1970s that the government owed them more than that. Veterans' groups wanted the U.S. government to pay disability compensation to Vietnam veterans suffering from diseases linked to Agent

Orange. Disability compensation is money given to veterans to live on if they cannot work because of their illnesses.

Veterans' organizations claimed that there was sufficient evidence linking exposure to Agent Orange to some kinds of cancer. They charged that the U.S. government was covering up the issue to avoid responsibility for the health of veterans exposed to Agent Orange.

But for more than ten years, the Veterans Administration (VA) of the U.S. government claimed that there was no conclusive evidence that Agent Orange caused cancer. It balked at honoring the more than thirty-four thousand Agent Orange claims that had been filed as of 1990. Finally in 1991, Congress voted to give permanent disability to veterans suffering from diseases caused by Agent Orange. The U.S. government's lack of cooperation over a ten-year period left veterans feeling betrayed and abandoned by the very government they served.

Missing in Action

The Paris Peace Accords provided for an exchange of prisoners of war, or POWs, between the United States and Vietnam. Between February 12 and March 29, 1973, 591 American prisoners were released by the North Vietnamese government. Families traveled to the bases where the freed POWs touched down once again on American soil and welcomed their loved ones home. Hugs were exchanged and tears fell as families that had been separated for as long as eight and a half years were at last reunited.

The return of the American POWs was one of the happier moments in an otherwise unhappy war. But many soldiers still have not come home from Vietnam. They are classified by the U.S. government as missing in action (MIA). In 1991, Gen. John W. Vessey (Ret.), the president's special emissary to Hanoi, estimated that approximately twenty-two hundred soldiers are still missing in action. Most are presumed to have died in action.

Yet, nearly twenty years after the U.S. withdrawal, rumors persist that Americans are still being held as POWs by the Vietnamese. The notion is so popular that many books have been written about the subject, and movies such as *Missing in Action* (1984) were made about returning to Vietnam to free POWs.

Vietnam veteran Adrian Fisch of St. James, Minnesota, began collecting information about MIAs in 1970. In 1991, Fisch remained convinced: "There's no question that there are Americans living in Vietnam as POWs. How to effect their return is another question. I doubt that our government will let that happen." Fisch believes that the government will not admit that the POWs exist because if "one American comes out, the country will go nuts. If one comes out, you have to explain all the rest. The majority of the information that we would like to get is still

Vietnam in the Movies

More than one hundred movies have been made that in one way or another touch on the Vietnam War. A sampling of a few of the important Vietnam movies documents the evolution of America's changing opinion of the war and its meaning.

Hollywood initally portrayed Vietnam as any other war. The producer and star of *The Green Berets* (1968) was actor John Wayne, a veteran of dozens of westerns and war movies. The movie treated Vietnam as a conflict similar to World War II and added some Cold War attitudes for good measure. The U.S. Special Forces soldiers were the good guys, who fought heroically to save South Vietnam from the Communist bad guys. The movie was released during the same year as the Tet Offensive, a time when Americans were learning just how complex the war really was. Film critics blasted the film for oversimplifying the issues of the war and glorifying America's role in it.

The movie Apocalypse Now *tried to depict the complex moral issues of war.*

Americans no longer tolerated the simple good guy-bad guy interpretations it had accepted in movies about World War II.

The Vietnam War had been over for nearly five years when a trio of antiwar movies was released that both reflected and influenced Americans' feelings about the war. *Coming Home* (1978) was one of the first major movies to examine the Vietnam War in a more complex way. Vietnam soldiers were not portrayed as heroes but as men who returned from Vietnam angry, bitter, and confused about their experiences. In one scene, Luke Martin, a paraplegic veteran played by actor Jon Voight, and a marine officer each talk about the war to an assembly of high school students. The marine officer's traditional, patriotic speech lays the groundwork for the movie's antiwar message. Luke Martin's emotional descriptions of seeing his friends mutilated and how it feels to kill someone still tug at the hearts of moviegoers. As Martin encourages the student to reject the simple, patriotic view of war given by the Marine, he speaks to everyone in the audience and cautions them to remember that war is neither simple nor glorifying. When it was released, *Coming Home* was praised by both audiences and critics. But viewed today, the movie may seem as oversimplified and preachy as *The Green Berets.*

The Deer Hunter (1979) viewed the war through the eyes of Michael, a blue-collar man typical of the millions of young men who served in Vietnam. Michael goes to Vietnam eager to serve his country, sees horrible and ugly things there, and returns home with a deeper understanding of the importance of life. His war experience makes him stop hunting deer. In contrast to *Coming Home,* this movie makes the important point that not all Vietnam soldiers returned home scarred and emotionally disturbed. Although its antiwar message is unmistakable, the movie seems less angry and more reflective about the war than *Coming Home*. It anticipates the general theme of the next wave of movies about the war.

The term "apocalypse" refers to religious writings about the destruction of evil and the triumph of good. Good versus evil is the theme of *Apocalypse Now* (1979). In the movie, Captain Willard, a U.S. Special Forces officer, is sent into the jungle to kill Colonel Kurz, a renegade American colonel. But Willard begins to admire Kurz and has trouble carrying out his mission. The movie blurs the concepts of good and evil, making it difficult to tell which is which. It seems to accurately reflect the complex moral issues the real war presents to America. Although there is no final statement about the morality of war, few moviegoers emerge from watching *Apocalypse Now* with a positive view of America's experience in Vietnam.

After *Apocalypse Now,* a new wave of films began to appear that reexamined Vietnam from a more distant perspective. Much of the initial anger America had felt about Vietnam had subsided, and Americans seemed interested in what really happened in Vietnam. Like earlier movies, the new crop of reexamination movies used soldiers as a focal point. *Hamburger Hill* (1984) and *Platoon* (1986) viewed the war through the eyes of the grunts who fought it. Actual Vietnam veterans praised both movies on how accurately they portrayed combat, living conditions, and the fears that preyed upon the minds of the grunts who served in the war. These and similar movies did much to identify America's shabby treatment of its Vietnam veterans and help restore their sense of dignity.

At about the same time, however, another group of movies ignored reality altogether and fought the Vietnam War all over again. This time Hollywood secured the victory that had originally eluded the United States. In *Missing in Action* (1984), Col. James Braddock, portrayed by actor Chuck Norris, returns to Vietnam in search of American POWs rumored to be held there. Braddock is portrayed as a superhero capable of defeating the enemy single-handedly. This movie, along with the *Rambo* series starring Sylvester Stallone, turned Vietnam veterans into Saturday morning cartoon heroes who bore no resemblance to real veterans. Despite the fact that these action movies offered little perspective on Vietnam and once again glorified warfare, they were immensely popular among mostly male moviegoers.

But *Missing in Action* and movies like it also gave voice to important themes. Braddock's return to Vietnam seemed to illustrate that America recognized it still had to deal with war issues it had been avoiding. The fact that he went back and won seemed to indicate a need in America to rewrite the Vietnam War experience in a more comfortable way.

Movies like Missing in Action *glorified war and turned Vietnam veterans into Saturday morning cartoon heroes.*

classified and locked in government files. It is considered [by the government] as a danger to national security. [But] It's a danger to national embarrassment."

In 1991, General Vessey was skeptical of the rumors about live Americans held in Vietnam, but he refused to discount them. "The Vietnamese have maintained since 1973 that they have not held live Americans. No recently dated evidence suggests that there are live Americans held in captivity. About 2,200 live sighting [reports] have been investigated and disproved. The likelihood [of live POWs in Vietnam] is far less than even three and a half years ago. [Verification] will continue to get harder as people get older, and witnesses die."

Despite the disagreement over the live POW question, both the U.S. government and those who believe POWs are still alive in Vietnam continued efforts to obtain what two presidents have called "the fullest possible accounting" for those men who are missing in action. But some of the MIA cases will never be solved because between four and five hundred bodies were lost at sea. The bodies of other missing Americans may have been blown to pieces by bombs or mines, making recovery of their remains impossible.

The MIA issue leaves part of the Vietnam War unfinished. For the families of soldiers still missing in action, the war has never ended. They continue to hope that one day the fate of their loved ones will be learned.

Vietnamese Refugees

As the city of Saigon fell to the Communists in the spring of 1975, South Vietnamese people who had served in military or government positions fled the country. They left to escape imprisonment or even execution by the North Vietnamese. The North Vietnamese viewed anyone who had ties to the South Vietnamese or American governments as a threat to their new government.

Many Americans believed the United States owed a special debt to these refugees because the United States had abandoned South Vietnam in 1973. During 1975, 130,000 people fled Vietnam in the days following the fall of the South Vietnamese government. Most of them were resettled in the United States. For the next three years, a stream of refugees flowed out of Vietnam. Approximately 30,000 more refugees left Vietnam and most found new homes in America.

In mid-1978, the stream of refugees turned into a flood. The Communist government instituted harsh policies against Vietnamese people of Chinese ancestry. By mid-1979, more than 200,000 additional Vietnamese had fled. They became known as boat people because they left Vietnam in small, leaky boats that were barely seaworthy.

Vietnamese citizens fleeing Vietnam seek entry to Hong Kong in 1989. There were about three hundred people who sailed into port aboard five boats.

To address the plight of the boat people, a conference of sixty-five nations gathered in Geneva, Switzerland, in July 1979. The conference decided that the nations of Southeast Asia would serve as a first asylum, providing temporary homes for the boat people. Western nations like the United States, Great Britain, Australia, France, and Canada would provide permanent homes for them. The Vietnamese government was pressured to improve conditions within the country so that its citizens would not be so eager to leave.

But in 1986, the number of boat people fleeing from Vietnam began to rise again. A second conference was held in Geneva in 1989. The nations participating in the conference were no longer open about accepting new refugees. Because every refugee left relatives behind who also wanted to escape from Vietnam, there seemed to be no end in sight to the problem.

The first asylum countries of Southeast Asia wanted to sharply reduce the number of boat people that they accepted.

The conference decided to interview each Vietnamese refugee and allow only those who were deemed political refugees to immigrate. The rest would be sent back to Vietnam. The conference left many Vietnamese people with little hope of leaving Vietnam for a new life in another country.

The U.S. position on the boat people is unclear. In a speech at the 1989 conference, Secretary of State Lawrence Eagleburger said that the United States opposed the concept of forcing refugees to return to Vietnam, where they would be viewed as criminals and imprisoned. But in the same speech, Eagleburger said that the United States would not "seek to alter" the conference's plans to interview refugees and send many of them back to Vietnam.

Today many Vietnamese refugees are stranded in refugee camps awaiting permanent resettlement. Thousands of Vietnamese wish to leave the oppressive rule of their homeland behind and find new homes where they can live in peace. These hapless refugees remain a significant problem for the United States and many other nations around the world as well.

Many Vietnamese refugees remain stranded in refugee camps awaiting permanent resettlement. This man, photographed in a Hong Kong refugee camp in 1989, is one of many such refugees.

A Vietnamese Refugee's Story

Chi Lu is one of the thousands of refugees who was forced to flee from South Vietnam and come to the United States. Lu worked for the South Vietnamese Ministry of Labor as director general of training and employment. His job was to build a center to provide training for the 200,000 troops who would soon leave the military and return to private life, as the Paris Peace Accords directed.

In late April 1975, as sporadic gunfire sounded around the city of Saigon, Lu knew his life and the lives of his family were in danger. "If the Communists took power, there would be a bloodbath. Anyone with U.S. ties was viewed by the North Vietnamese as an agent for the CIA [Central Intelligence Agency]. If I stayed, I knew that I would be imprisoned or killed."

On April 28, Lu was able to get his wife and nine children on a plane out of Saigon. Their destination was Faribault, Minnesota, in the United States. His wife's younger sister had married an American from Faribault, and they had agreed to sponsor them. Lu remained behind, unable to get on a plane.

That night Communist rocket fire exploded around Saigon as the attack on the city began. Lu saw gas and oil fires burning around the city.

Lu returned to the airport and met a Vietnamese student who was studying in the United States and who had returned to Saigon to help members of his family escape. By pretending to be the young man's father-in-law, Lu was able to get on one of the last planes that left the Saigon airport before the city fell to the Communists.

The Lu family started life over again in Faribault with nothing. The local welfare office gave the entire family of eleven only $200 a month in assistance. Lu, a former high government official, took a job as a clerk in a department store for $2.54 per hour. In 1976, he took a new job in a factory as a quality control inspector and also continued to work part time at the department store. For the next three years, Lu worked nearly every day, with no weekends off. Through hard work and help from friends, Lu was eventually able to buy a house in Faribault.

Later he moved to a suburb of St. Paul, Minnesota. He became director of Vietnam Social Services, an organization that helps Vietnamese come to America and adjust to American life.

But his new life in America is not the same as living in his own country. "I feel very sorry about leaving my homeland. We think of the cemeteries of our families and send gifts back to friends in Vietnam to help rebuild them. God willing, if peace comes to Vietnam and the Communists are gone, I will be among the first Vietnamese to return to Vietnam."

Chi Lu points to a map of Vietnam as he recounts his harrowing escape.

Continued Fighting

The fall of South Vietnam did not end the fighting in Southeast Asia. About the same time that the Saigon government fell, the government of Cambodia was also overthrown by Communists. But a split soon developed between the new Cambodian government and the newly united Vietnam. The new Cambodian government brutally suppressed any opposition within the country, killing thousands of people. The new government also demanded the return of land seized by the Vietnamese centuries earlier and launched numerous attacks against Vietnam along the border between the two countries.

In 1978, Vietnam retaliated with an invasion of Cambodia. The Vietnamese overthrew the existing Communist government in Cambodia and replaced it with a new pro-Vietnam Communist government. For several years afterward, occupation forces remained inside Cambodia.

Vietnam was universally condemned for its invasion and occupation of Cambodia. In numerous ways, Vietnam's intervention in Cambodian affairs and the protests it raised from other countries was similar to America's intervention in Vietnam. To describe the dilemma Vietnam found itself in, the news media sometimes referred to the invasion as Vietnam's Vietnam.

What happened in Cambodia has become part of the United States' Vietnam legacy. The invasion revived the debate among Americans over the morality of U.S. withdrawal from Vietnam in 1973. The bloodshed in Cambodia served as an example of what might happen if the United States did not continue its self-appointed role as the policeman of the free world. Many Americans who had initially cheered the U.S. withdrawal from Vietnam now wonder if the United States could have prevented the bloodshed in Cambodia by maintaining its presence in Vietnam. From now on, when U.S. leaders face foreign policy decisions, they must weigh the fear of falling into "another Vietnam" against the fear of allowing "another Cambodia."

Avoiding Another Vietnam

The United States "lost" the Vietnam War because it had the wrong goals, used the wrong military strategy and employed weapons that proved ineffective in the end. Perhaps most importantly, the United States failed in Vietnam because the war lost support among the American people. Americans and their leaders continue to study America's failures in Vietnam in an effort to avoid repeating them in the future.

Many Americans point to the Persian Gulf War as proof that the United States has learned from its military mistakes in Vietnam. In 1990, Iraq invaded its neighbor Kuwait. U.S. President

George Bush called for Iraq to withdraw from Kuwait and promised to use force if necessary to make Iraq leave.

The promise to use U.S. troops overseas made many Americans apprehensive and fearful of falling into another Vietnam. But Bush avoided two major military mistakes that Johnson made. Unlike Vietnam, the United States avoided a slow escalation of the Gulf War. U.S. forces were built up in advance rather than over a period of years. The military did not fight only to avoid defeat, as it had in Vietnam. This time the military focused on a clear military goal: Drive Iraq out of Kuwait. The United States achieved its goal in less than two months.

Some observers note that the Gulf War also showed that Americans had learned a lesson from Vietnam about how to treat its veterans. Although Americans may not entirely have supported the U.S. position in the Gulf War, they did not hold veterans responsible for it, as they had done in Vietnam. Returning soldiers were welcomed home as heroes and remembered with parties and parades.

Others argue that the best lesson of the Vietnam War may be the simple fact that it happened. Regardless of their views on the

Kuwaiti citizens celebrated the liberation of their nation with parades. Americans—mindful of how they treated veterans of the Vietnam War—welcomed U.S. soldiers returning from the Persian Gulf War.

war, Americans are united on one thing about Vietnam: Almost everyone wants to avoid another experience like it. In every world crisis that arises where a U.S. commitment might be necessary, politicians, the media, and the people warn their leaders that they do not want the situation to turn into another Vietnam. In 1991, for example, President Bush promised America that U.S. involvement in the Persian Gulf would not be another Vietnam. If the lessons of the Vietnam War can remain in the consciousness of America, the nation may never again have to experience such a national nightmare.

Rewriting History

Although the Vietnam War has been over for nearly twenty years, understanding its lasting significance has only begun. Americans still react emotionally to Vietnam, and their conclusions about Vietnam are often guided as much by their emotions as by facts. In the future, new interpretations of Vietnam's lessons may be written.

By continually reevaluating the war and its aftermath in light of the changing times, future historians will be able to explain the Vietnam legacy more fully. In the future, Vietnam may be remembered less as a lost war. Vietnam might be remembered more for the hard lessons that were learned by America, its leaders, and its people.

Glossary

Agent Orange a chemical the United States sprayed on the South Vietnamese countryside to defoliate trees and destroy crops.

cold war the conflict that characterized the hostilities between the Communist Soviet Union and the democratic United States between 1945 and 1988.

colonialism the system by which one country establishes control over distant territories for the purpose of economic gain.

communism a government in which all property is owned by the state. The spread of communism by the governments of the Soviet Union, China, and North Vietnam was viewed in the 1950s and 1960s by the United States as a threat to its national security.

Demilitarized Zone or **DMZ** buffer area along the seventeenth parallel border between North and South Vietnam formalized by the Geneva Accords of 1954.

Dien Bien Phu city held by the French forces and attacked by North Vietnam in 1954. The eventual surrender of the French at Dien Bien Phu brought France's century-long rule of Vietnam to an end.

domino theory a theory that if one country fell to communism, surrounding countries would soon follow.

draft the selection of men for required service in a country's armed forces.

Gulf of Tonkin incident two attacks by North Vietnamese gunboats on American ships in the Gulf of Tonkin off the coast of North Vietnam on August 2 and 4, 1964. The events led to the passage of the Gulf of Tonkin Resolution by the U.S. Congress, which allowed President Johnson to escalate U.S. involvement in Vietnam.

Ho Chi Minh Trail a North Vietnamese supply route to South Vietnam that wound through the neighboring countries of Laos and Cambodia.

legacy anything that is handed down from one generation to the next.

MIA missing in action; a term used to describe soldiers who cannot be accounted for during wartime.

nationalism the desire within a country for independence from foreign rule.

national security protection of a nation from attack or harm by another nation.

posttraumatic stress disorder or **PTSD** an emotional condition in war veterans caused by the delayed reaction to combat.

POW an abbreviation for prisoner of war, a term used to describe prisoners taken during wartime.

Spring Offensive a military campaign launched by North Vietnam against South Vietnam in the spring of 1972.

Tet Offensive a military campaign launched early in 1968 by North Vietnam against South Vietnam. Tet was the turning point in America's involvement in the Vietnam War.

Vietcong Communist-supported revolutionaries who sought to overthrow the South Vietnamese government.

Vietminh Communist-supported revolutionaries who sought to overthrow the South Vietnamese government. Name changed to Vietcong after about 1960.

Vietnamization the process of withdrawing U.S. troops from South Vietnam and replacing them with South Vietnamese troops.

war of attrition a war where one side tries to win by destroying the other side's supplies and troops until it can no longer fight.

Key Individuals in the Vietnam War

William L. Calley Jr. American serviceman who led the killings of South Vietnamese villagers at My Lai.

Clark Clifford U.S. secretary of defense, 1968–69; told President Johnson that further escalation of U.S. involvement in Vietnam would be pointless.

Ngo Dinh Diem leader of South Vietnam from 1954 to 1963. His harsh rule angered South Vietnamese peasants and gave the Communists a starting point to spread the revolution in the south. Diem was assassinated in 1963 by members of the army. The assassination plot had the approval of the United States.

Dwight D. Eisenhower president of the United States (1953–1961). He supported the French involvement in Vietnam and in 1954 used the term "domino theory" publicly for the first time.

Vo Nguyen Giap commander of North Vietnamese army that defeated the French at Dien Bien Phu. He continued the campaign against South Vietnam, including the Tet Offensive in 1968 and the Spring Offensive in 1972.

Lyndon B. Johnson American president (1963–1969) who escalated U.S. involvement in the Vietnam conflict.

John F. Kennedy president of the United States (1961–1963). Kennedy committed U.S. political and military advisers to South Vietnam. He is rumored to have approved the plot to assassinate Diem. Kennedy himself was assassinated on November 22, 1963.

Henry Kissinger special assistant and later secretary of state under Richard Nixon. He negotiated Paris Accords that disengaged the United States from the Vietnam conflict.

Ho Chi Minh Vietnamese leader credited as the most influential in Vietnam's efforts to gain independence from France. Ho helped organize the Communist party in Vietnam in 1930. In 1946, he became leader of North Vietnam and successfully campaigned to drive the French out of Vietnam in 1954. He died in 1969, six years before the fall of South Vietnam and the reunification of Vietnam.

Richard Nixon American president (1969–1974) who Vietnamized the war and eventually disengaged the United States from the Vietnam conflict in 1973.

Nguyen Van Thieu president of South Vietnam (1967–1975). His harsh and unfair policies encouraged many South Vietnamese to support the Communist revolution. He ordered the retreat from the northern provinces, which started the collapse of South Vietnam in 1975. Thieu fled Saigon just before it fell.

Le Duc Tho North Vietnamese representative, who, with Henry Kissinger of the United States, negotiated the Paris Peace Accords in 1973.

Harry S Truman president of the United States (1945–1953). He developed the containment of communism policy that eventually led to the U.S. political and military involvement in Vietnam.

William C. Westmoreland U.S. commander in Vietnam (1964–1968). Westmoreland planned the war of attrition strategy that failed in Vietnam.

For Further Reading

Lady Borton, *Sensing the Enemy: An American Woman Among the Boat People of Vietnam*. Garden City, NY: Dial Press, 1986.

Judy Donnelly, *A Wall of Names: The Story of the Vietnam Veterans Memorial*. New York: Random House, 1991.

William Dudley and David Bender, eds. *The Vietnam War: Opposing Viewpoints,* 2nd Ed. San Diego: Greenhaven Press, 1990.

Bob Green, *Homecoming: When the Soldiers Returned from Vietnam*. New York: G.P. Putnam's Sons, 1989.

Denis J. Hauptly, *In Vietnam*. New York: Atheneum, 1985.

Don Lawson, *An Album of the Vietnam War*. New York: Franklin Watts, 1986.

Don Lawson, *The United States in the Vietnam War*. New York: Thomas Y. Crowell, 1981.

Harry Nickelson, *Vietnam*. San Diego: Lucent Books, Inc., 1989.

Charles Wills, *The Tet Offensive*. Englewood Cliffs, NJ: Silver Burdett Press, Inc., 1989.

David K. Wright, *Vietnam*. Chicago: Childrens Press, 1988.

David K. Wright, *War in Vietnam,* (Books I-IV). Chicago: Children's Press, 1988.

Works Consulted

This is only a partial listing of the works consulted by the author.

Books

Brian Beckett, *Illustrated History of the Vietnam War*. New York: Gallery Books, 1985.

David L. Bender, *The Vietnam War: Opposing Viewpoints*. St. Paul: Greenhaven Press, 1984.

Lt. Gen. Phillip B. Davidson (USA Ret.), *Vietnam at War, The History 1946-75*. Novato, CA: Presidio Press, 1988.

James Pinckney Harrison, *The Endless War: Fifty Years of Struggle in Vietnam*. New York: The Free Press, A Division of Macmillan Publishing Co., Inc., 1982.

William Homolka, *Americans in Southeast Asia: The POW/MIA Issue*. New York: New World Books, 1986.

Marvin Kalb and Elie Abel, *Roots of Involvement: The U.S. in Asia 1784-1971*. New York: W. W. Norton & Company Inc., 1971.

Gabriel Kolko, *Anatomy of a War: Vietnam, the United States and the Modern Historical Experience*. New York: Pantheon Books, 1985.

Robert Emmet Long, ed., *Vietnam Ten Years After*. New York: The H.W. Wilson Company, 1986.

John Clark Pratt, *Vietnam Voices: Perspectives on the War Years, 1941-1982*. New York: Viking, 1984.

Harrison E. Salisbury, ed., *Vietnam Reconsidered: Lessons from a War*. New York: Harper & Row, 1984.

William S. Turley, *The Second IndoChina War, A Short Political and Military History, 1954-75*. Boulder, CO: Westview Press, 1986.

U.S. Government, Department of the Army, *Vietnam: A Country Study*, (Area Handbook Series). Washington, D.C.: 101.22:550-32, 1989.

Periodicals

The American Legion, "Agent Orange," c. 1990 (articles extracted from *American Legion* magazine).

Steve Bentley, "A Short History of PTSD," *Veteran,* vol. 11, no. 1, January 1991.

Joseph L. Galloway, "Vietnam Story," *U.S. News & World Report,* vol. 109, no. 17, October 1990.

Rob Jones, "Vietnam on the Silver Screen," *Vietnam,* vol. 11. Issue 1, February 1986.

Lori Kenepp, "Ways to Look at PTSD," *Veteran,* January 1991.

Bill McCloud, "What Should We Tell Our Children About Vietnam?" *American Heritage,* May/June 1988.

Index

Agent Orange, 95
    effect on veterans, 94
    use of by U.S. in Vietnam, 34
American Embassy
    evacuation of, 87-88
Americans
    Vietnam and
        changing opinion about, 63-64
        disappointment over loss in, 89-90
        divided opinions about, 53, 55, 58
        impact of Vietnam War on, 7
        opposition to Vietnam War, 48
        reaction to My Lai, 75
        trust in government and, 90-91
An Loc
    battle of, 78
Apocalypse Now, 97
attrition
    U.S. decision to fight a war of, 28

Ban Me Thuot
    communist victory at, 86
Bao Dai
    as French nominee to lead Vietnam, 16
battles
    between U.S. forces and North Vietnam
        as stalemates, 38, 40-41
    traditional
        as U.S. strength, 37
Berrigan, Daniel and Philip
    Vietnam protests of, 56
blacks
    civil rights demands of, 50
    discrimination against, 54
boat people, 99
    U.S. position toward, 100
booby traps
    North Vietnamese, 33
boycott of bus lines in Alabama, 54
Bush, George, 102
    promise to avoid another Vietnam, 103-104

Calley, William, Jr.
    involvement in My Lai, 75
Cambodia
    attempt to overthrow communist government, 102
    government of
        violation of civil rights and, 102
    invasion of, 71-72
        increased antiwar protests, 72
    secret bombings of, 69, 71
        announcement of, 72
Canada
    draft dodgers flee to, 61
Cantonsville Nine
    trial of, 56
capitalism
    compared to communism, 9-10
Carmichael, Stokely

advocate of violence, 54
cease-fire agreement
    violation of, 83-84
Chi Lu
    story of, 101
China, 11
    improvements in relationship with, 68
    increased trade with, 76
    military aid to Vietminh, 16
    U.S. fear of involvement in Vietnam, 27
Christmas bombings
    unpopularity of, 82
Citadel
    attack on, 46
Civil Rights Act (1964), 54
civil rights movement, 50
    description of, 54
civil rights, Vietnamese
    as suppressed by French, 11
Civil War, U.S., 54, 89
    compared to Vietnam War, 7
Clifford, Clark, 47
cold war
    beginning of, 10
Coming Home
    portrayal of Vietnam veterans in, 96
communism
    as reason for Vietnam War, 7
    as threat to U.S., 10
    description of, 9-10
    protesters' objection to, 55
conscientious objectors
    description of, 61
containment policy, 10
credibility gap
    creation of, 64

Deer Hunter, The, 96-97
Demilitarized Zone, 17
democracy
    as goal of U.S. foreign policy, 10
Democratic Republic of Vietnam
    formation of, 14-15
detente, 77
    Nixon's strategy for peace, 76
    purposes of, 76
Dien Bien Phu
    siege of, 17
discrimination
    draft as form of, 58
    prevalence of, 54
domino theory
    description of, 10, 22
doves
    antiwar demonstrators, 53
    early protests of, 55
    influence on foreign policy, 55
draft
    as target for protesters, 58
    board offices
        defiling of as protests, 56
    cards, burning of, 60

criticisms of
    as discriminatory, 58
    military
        reasons for, 58-59
    support of
        as dividing Americans, 60-61
    ways to avoid, 61
drug abuse
    among Vietnam veterans, 91
    in the fifties, 52
    increase of in the sixties, 52
    the sixties and, 49
Dylan, Bob, 49

Eagleburger, Lawrence, 100
Earley, Raymond
    Vietnam experiences of, 93-94
Eastern Europe
    Soviet takeover of, 10
economy, U.S.
    effect of Vietnam War on, 65
Eisenhower, Dwight
    development of domino theory, 22
elections
    in South Vietnam
        cancellation of, 20
        provisions for in Vietnam War, 18
Emspak, Frank, 57
escalation of Vietnam War, 55
Establishment, The, 49
Evers, Medgar
    assassination of, 54

Fisch, Adrian, 95
Ford, Gerald R., 86
France
    granted Vietnam independence, 16
    involvement in Vietnam, 11-14
        growing weary of, 17
        proposal of diplomacy, 17
        recognition of DRV, 15
        reinstitution of colonial rule, 15
        repression of civil rights, 11
        U.S. aid to, 22
French Foreign Legion, 13

generation gap, 52
Geneva Accords
    results of, 17-18
Geneva Conference
    discussion of Vietnamese refugees, 99-100
Great Society
    description of, 30
Greece
    U.S. involvement in, 10
Green Berets
    as traditional war movie, 96
guerrilla warfare, Vietnamese, 32-34
Gulf of Tonkin incident, 22, 25
    controversy surrounding, 24
Gulf of Tonkin Resolution
    passage of, 25

repeal of, 69, 74
Hair, 51
hawks
  influence on foreign policy, 55
  organized rallies of, 58
  war supporters, 53
helicopter
  importance in Vietnam War, 31
herbicides
  used by U.S., 34
hippies, 49
Ho Chi Minh, 12, 13
  ability to rally peasant support, 12
  as president of Democratic Republic of Vietnam, 14-15
  return to Vietnam, 14
Ho Chi Minh Trail
  description of, 29
  inability for U.S. to shut down, 28, 29
Hue
  Vietcong attack on, 46

Indochinese Communist Party, 13
Iraq
  invasion of Kuwait, 102

Japan
  invasion of Vietnam, 14
Johnson, Lyndon B., 25, 47
  as advocate of Great Society, 30
  as president, 23
  decision to keep fighting, 41
  decision to send troops to Vietnam, 27
  increase in involvement in Vietnam, 53
  lies about war effort, 62, 64
  loss of public support, 62, 65
  most Americans supported in 1965, 53
  possible involvement in Gulf of Tonkin, 24
  refusal to seek reelection, 66
  use of domino theory, 22
  Vietnam policies, inconsistency in, 55
  violation of public trust, 90

Kennedy, John F.
  assassination of, 23, 49
  election of, 49
  escalation of involvement in Vietnam, 20-21
Kent State
  description of, 73
Khe Sanh
  U.S. retaliatory attacks on, 41-43
  Vietcong attack on, 41
King, Martin Luther, Jr., 50
  active in civil rights movement, 54
  assassination of, 54
Kissinger, Henry, 79
Kolko, Gabriel, 40
Korea, 10-11
Korean War, 89

Lam Son 719 Campaign, 74-75

effect of, 76
Laos
  invasion of, 74-76
Le Duc Tho, 79, 81
League for the Independence of Vietnam, 14
"Leave It to Beaver," 51
limited war
  decision to fight, 27
    disadvantages to, 28, 32
    Nixon's strategy to revoke, 71
love, free, 49
LSD
  use of in sixties, 52

Maddox, USS
  attack on, 25
Malcolm X, 50
marijuana
  use of in sixties, 52
marriage
  rejection of, 50
Martin, Graham, 87
Mason, Jim, 41, 89
  battle experiences of, 39
Maya Ying Lin, 92
media
  publication of Watergate scandal, 86
  Vietnam War and
    impact on public opinion, 63-64, 91
    publicizing of antiwar demonstrations, 65
MIAs, 95
  controversy surrounding, 95, 98
Miller, David, 60
Missing in Action, 95, 97
movies
  role in reexamining Vietnam War, 97
  Vietnam, 96-97
My Lai massacre, 75

napalm
  use of by U.S. in Vietnam, 34
National Association of Colored People (NAACP), 54
National Coordinating Committee to End the War in Vietnam, 57
National Guard
  antiwar protests and, 72-74
  shooting of students at Kent State, 73
negotiations, peace
  proposal for, 65-66
Ngo Dinh Diem
  assassination of, 23
  ineptness of, 19
  president of South Vietnam, 18
  torture of peasants, 42
Nguyen Van Thieu
  declaration of martial law, 45
  rejection of peace talks, 80
  retreat of, 86, 87
  unpopularity of, 42, 84-86
  U.S. aid to, 81
Nixon, Richard
  decision to end limited war, 71

detente and, 76
  election of, 68
  ignores Congress, 74
  proposal for an honorable peace, 68
    details of, 68-70
  rejection of Paris Peace Talk agreement, 81
  violation of public trust, 91
  Watergate and, 69, 86
  withdrawal of U.S. troops and, 70, 76
North Vietnam (Democratic Republic of Vietnam)
  agreement to attend peace talks, 67
  attacks on South Vietnam, 78
  bombing campaign of, 82
  communist takeover in, 15
  compared to United States, 32
  creation of, 18
  goal of
    compared to U.S., 34-35
  Nixon's attempt to destroy, 72
  strategy of, 35
  use of Ho Chi Minh Trail, 29

Operation Phoenix
  failure of, 42-43

Paris Peace Accords
  prisoners of war and, 95
  delays in, 67-68
  improvements in, 79-80
  Kissinger and, 79
  proposal for, 65-66
  renegotiation of, 81-82
  results of, 80
  treaty
    signing of, 82-83
peaceniks, 55
peasants
  dislike of U.S., 42
  importance of winning support of, 14, 42
  support of Vietcong, 20
Persian Gulf War
  compared to Vietnam, 7, 102-103
  difference in treatment of veterans, 103
posttraumatic stress disorder
  definition of, 91-93
poverty
  war on in U.S., 30
prisoners of war, 95
  controversy surrounding, 95, 98
  sightings of, 98
protest movement, Vietnam
  early protests, 55
  escalation of, 57
  formation of a national organization, 57
  increasing support for, 64-65
  objections of
    moral and political, 55
  response to escalation, 55
  response to Cambodian invasion, 72
public trust
  erosion of, 90-91

Photo Credits

Cover photo by The Bettmann Archive

AP/Wide World Photos, 12, 13, 16 (both), 19, 20 (both), 21, 23, 25, 26 (both), 29, 30, 34 (all), 35, 36, 40 (top), 41, 44, 46, 48 (top), 50, 54, 55, 56, 59, 62, 68, 69, 72, 74, 75, 78, 80, 81, 83 (top two), 84, 85, 87 (bottom), 92, 93, 94, 99, 100, 103

Roger Barr, 101

Hollywood Book and Poster, 96, 97

Lyndon B. Johnson Library, 47 (bottom right)

National Archives, 11, 15, 17, 28, 31, 33 (right), 37 (all), 38 (both), 39, 42 (both), 43 (top), 47 (left and top right), 48 (bottom), 63, 64, 70, 71 (both), 82 (right), 83 (bottom), 90

National Portrait Gallery, 22, 24

Smithsonian, 82 (left)

© 1990 Martha Swope, 51

Harry S Truman Library, 10

UPI/Bettmann Newsphotos, 18, 32, 33 (left), 40 (bottom), 43 (bottom), 45, 51, 52, 57, 60, 73, 79, 87 (top), 88

About the Author

Roger Barr is a free-lance writer, editor, and publishing consultant who lives in St. Paul, Minnesota. He grew up during the Vietnam War and regularly wrote letters to his brother who served in Vietnam in 1968. He has written several articles about the war. Through personal experience and research, he has learned that it is easier to ask questions about the war than it is to answer them.